Shipping

Homes

The Blueprint to Build Your Sustainable Dream House Exactly the Way You Want It. Including the DIY Techniques You Need Explained Step-by-Step, Plans and Design Ideas

Oliver Tomecek

Table of Content

Introduction

In the 1950s, Malcolm McLean developed the shipping container. This innovation has revolutionized the transportation industry by offering bulk delivery efficiently and cost-effectively. Shipping containers are sturdy corrugated steel boxes that can be loaded and moved with cargo. To date, they are widely available worldwide.

However, it took another three decades before filing the first patent for turning shipping containers into habitable buildings. The idea was novel, and it had far-reaching implications. For a cheap cost and in a short period of time, these strong, widely accessible containers may be transformed into homes, schools, companies, even residential complexes or sports stadiums.

Throughout recent decades, the use of shipping container homes for commercial and residential purposes has become more widespread in Europe. They construct emergency shelters, overcrowding housing, shopping malls, schools, and a range of other structures. Because shipping containers may be modified in any way, they are perfect for various applications. They may be modified to suit the needs of any structure.

Shipping containers aren't only used as dwelling quarters in Europe. People in need all around the world have benefited from these readily available materials, which have offered sustainable and affordable architecture. As a consequence of the growing need for green, low-cost, and long-term building solutions, shipping container architecture has become a global phenomenon. Anyone may now build their own unique and beautiful home, customized to their own requirements and finished in less time and with less expense that traditional homes take.

There are many advantages to building and living in shipping container homes. As previously said, they are structurally solid, inexpensive, and long-lasting. They could save a lot of energy, as the United States alone has approximately 50 million extra shipping containers. With so many individuals trying to find affordable housing in today's market, these sturdy, well-built structures may be a viable alternative to traditional homes.

Listed below are a few of the benefits of shipping container homes:

Quick to construct - Instead of taking months to construct conventional houses, shipping container homes may be constructed in only a few days.

Environmentally friendly - Instead of using bricks, cement, or wood to construct the shell of your house, shipping containers provide a prefabricated shell with little environmental effect. Even the shipping container itself is cost-effective since it recycles materials that would otherwise be thrown away.

Extremely durable - Anyone who has seen a cargo container knows how durable they are. They're constructed of Corten steel, which can withstand a variety of conditions. During storms and warfare, shipping containers have been utilized as emergency shelters.

Affordable - This is a critical factor to consider. Traditional houses may cost hundreds of thousands of dollars, but a shipping container home can be built for as little as $14,000. This may vary depending on the changes made, the number of shipping containers utilized, and whether the house is constructed on your own or with the assistance of a contractor, but it is feasible to build and move into your home for a very low cost.

Transportable - While transporting a shipping container home after it has been put on the foundation is not easy, it is feasible and has been done many times. This is something that conventional houses just cannot accommodate.

It is always better to finish your homework before getting started with anything. We'll go through everything you need to know to acquire, alter, place, complete, and move into your shipping container house in this book. We'll go through every aspect with you and provide advice to assist you to prevent any delays or expensive errors.

Chapter 1
Understanding Shipping Container Homes

Shipping containers may be found almost everywhere in the globe, whether on trains, huge ships, or over-the-road vehicles driving down the highway. They're utilized for intermodal transportation and international commerce, as well as storage units, temporary structures, and, as we'll see, houses. Shipping containers can be loaded into a variety of means of transportation and placed on the ground with ease. They can transport a wide range of cargo and are in charge of the bulk of imported and exported products.

Shipping containers are available in various sizes. The most popular sizes for usage as a house are 20 feet to 40 feet in length. In order to lawfully drive along roads, containers must be at least 8 feet wide. This is a significant distinction from mobile houses, which may be up to 16 feet wide when transported with oversize permits. The interior height of shipping containers is approximately 8 feet, although high cube variants may reach closer to 912 feet. On average, they can carry 44,000 to 50,000 pounds of cargo. Locking brackets may be used to stack and lock shipping containers together. This explains why they may be seen double-piled on trains and stacked many containers high on ships.

1.1 The Appeal of Shipping Container Homes

A shipping container house is a relatively new idea around the globe. They've evolved into one of a slew of alternatives for individuals seeking a different kind of home. After the 2008 financial crisis, when expensive housing was heavily criticized, several signs of either the beginning of a significant increase in alternative housing can be found. Economic instability has loomed in the years following, as wages have remained stagnant and income inequality seems to be increasing.

As a result of these economic reasons, there has been an increase in demand for alternative housing. Because shipping container houses are unlike any other, they provide benefits that are difficult to obtain elsewhere.

Potential house buyers and builders may benefit from shipping container homes in a variety of ways. Aside from possible cost savings, shipping container houses may have a beneficial impact on the environment, provide robust exterior strength to defend against harsh weather, and can frequently be relocated once the inside is finished. Though shipping container houses have certain disadvantages, they provide benefits that are not usually seen in other kinds of housing.

Potential house owners who decide to build their own shipping container home may discover that there are financial advantages to doing so. Builders may tailor the house to include just the elements that are most important to them. They may select where to look for things and use resources that they are familiar with. The container provides a highly strong semi-complete construction almost instantly, which is a major benefit for a low budget customer. The finer features and more opulent improvements may be added when their money permits.

Many of today's young people are more ecologically aware than their elders. With this in mind, shipping container houses are attractive because they may offer existing containers a new lease on life as they reach the end of their useful lives. Though this is a contentious concept, since containers can be trashed and recycled, it may still be a good idea to reuse them in other ways. Furthermore, some purchasers will choose to maximize the container's robust metal shell rather than utilizing additional material to construct external wall surfaces. The size of a shipping container also forces many homeowners to downsize their possessions, perhaps lowering their environmental effect.

Hazardous weather may be a big issue depending on where you choose to put your shipping container house. Shipping container houses are very strong buildings that can survive severe weather such as hurricanes, tornadoes, and high winds. Onboard ocean boats in stormy seas, these containers are built to resist huge waves and wind gusts. They are intended to be watertight both to preserve the cargo within and to float if they fall overboard an ocean vessel, but they are not always dependable if not properly maintained. In a coastal region prone to storms or typhoons or in the flatlands prone to tornado outbreaks, shipping container houses may be an excellent low-cost housing alternative.

Despite the fact that mobile and modular houses have comparable benefits, shipping container homes may be relocated even after the interior construction is completed. The houses may occasionally be relocated to entirely new sites, needing just a new foundation and utility connections, depending on the particular design. As previously mentioned, the logistical expenses of transporting a shipping container home may be considerably cheaper since special oversize licenses are not required to drive along the road. Because shipping containers are so extensively utilized throughout the globe, there is a lot more equipment to move and transport them.

1.2 Shipping Container Home Drawbacks

Not all of the distinctive features of a shipping container house are beneficial. Others see some of the main characteristics that many views as benefits to be detrimental. While some individuals may appreciate the container's robust and solid exterior, others say that dealing with thick metal for doors, windows, and ventilation adds to the difficulty. Cutting through the metal skin requires specialized knowledge and equipment, as well as extra reinforcing once the cut is completed.

For others, the ease with which shipping containers may be relocated is also a point of contention. The fact that they are smaller than a mobile or modular house contributes to their capacity to be relocated easily. Is it really important if it's easy or not if you're not the one driving the truck down the road? Professional drivers can do the task in any case. Thus, the benefit is minor at best. This benefit or drawback may only be assessed by each individual homeowner in their particular circumstances.

As young people plan for their financial futures, it's essential to think about how a shipping container house will retain its worth in the future. While many people think they can preserve or even increase their worth in the property market, this limits your prospective purchasers to a smaller group. Regardless matter how well-designed or maintained shipping container houses are, they are not for everyone. Purchasing a house that is likely to depreciate or lose value may put shipping container home purchasers up for failure if they decide to relocate or invest in other properties.

Locating your shipping container house in a hot real estate market is a smart way to ensure that it increases in value. Because the containers do not need much room, you may purchase a small lot and develop the container for less than the cost of buying or constructing a new house. If the market remains hot, you may be able to sell your shipping container house for considerably more than you paid for it since individuals often enter a hot real estate market for a particular purpose and are in desperate need of housing alternatives.

Use a real estate expert to locate similar houses in the region where you want to construct, even if they are difficult to come by in certain places. Compare your budget to what they could have sold for to see whether they're financially viable and will appreciate in value over time. Look into other options for housing, such as mobile homes and various types of small dwellings.

Understanding the benefits and drawbacks of shipping container houses may help you make the best choice for you. The drawbacks are mostly limited to those who do not like this type of house. If you think it suits your taste, it will most certainly do so since there are many shipping container houses on the market today, and they are attracting a lot of attention. You'll have plenty of knowledge and ideas on how to use a shipping container house to suit your requirements, thanks to the numerous resources available, including this book.

Living in a shipping container house is a unique and thrilling experience! Remember to prepare carefully, but also to have fun on your quest to finding the right house for you. Those who criticize will be joined by those who applaud. You're not alone on your trip, and there are some really amazing shipping container houses out there. Let your imagination go and create something unique!

Chapter 2
Preparing Your Plan

You've formally decided that constructing a shipping container house is exactly what you want to accomplish at this stage in your journey. You don't want a cave, a mobile house, or a conventional home. You've considered the benefits and drawbacks, do your homework, and are confident in your decision to construct your own shipping container house.

To be sure to follow all of the necessary steps toward constructing your shipping container house, careful planning is essential. Many stages must be completed in a certain sequence, and skipping one may cause delays in progressing to the next. Planning is also essential for completing tasks properly. Skipping stages or failing to prepare properly may result in substandard building techniques that will cost money in the long run to fix. Thanks to this book You will be taken through a number of stages in a sequential manner. However, read each step carefully since some of them may need to be begun and completed at various times.

Before taking any action, it is recommended that you read the whole text. Take notes as you go along and make the most of them.

Apart from your own personal planning requirements, any other parties involved in the building process will need knowledge of your particular plans in order to provide you with the finest goods and services possible. To ensure that your planned home meets local rules and laws, local government and regulatory organizations may need blueprints prior to construction.

Plans don't have to be elaborate, rolled-up drawings with engineer and architectural marks. Simple checklists and example drawings may help many people keep their projects organized and on track. If you're doing this project on your own, the way you lay out your construction is entirely up to you. If you are married, have significant other, or another interested party, you must work with them to ensure that you both agree on the best course of action. Spend the additional time preparing now to avoid a big disaster down the line.

When considering a shipping container house, the first things to consider are the fundamentals. You should choose the container size you want, the number of containers you'll need, the location where you'll construct it, and a general concept of how you'll alter the containers. Look at the many examples of container homes in this book for ideas on how they can be arranged, connected together, and on interior and exterior architecture. If you'd like, continue your search on the internet for inspiration as well.

You should also start searching for a suitable building location. Don't buy a site until you've figured out your budget; instead, get a sense of what's out there and how it works with the style you've come up with.

Then it will be time to think about how you're going to organize your container. Especially if you're planning to choose for an economical project, keep in mind that you'll have to deal with small spaces. But with the information and advice you'll find in this guide, you'll be able to manage even the smallest spaces creatively, making them perfect for your needs.

Bedrooms are usually found towards the extremities of containers since they take up a lot of space. In most kitchens, there is just one row of cabinets and worktops. It's entirely up to you how you want to create your layout. RV and travel trailer designs are a popular source of inspiration for shipping container house floor plans. These trucks are almost identical in size to a shipping container house.

Make a mental note of any characteristics that are particularly essential to you. Make a notation in large bold characters if sliding glass doors or a gas range are non-negotiable for you. Go shopping at a hardware store to discover what kinds of in-home features are available. Make a list of the costs, the difficulty of the installation, and the equipment and supplies you'll need.

Some characteristics may require a few steps at the start, a few more in the middle, and even more at the conclusion. Knowing what characteristics you truly want ahead of time enables you to start searching for the right materials far ahead of time. Your preferred laminate flooring may be available one week and sold out the next. Some shops, particularly your local ones, will let you buy a certain material and have it held for you until you're ready to install it. They are aware that you are doing a large job on your own and will happily assist you.

2.1 Planning Financially

Shipping container houses may be far less expensive than conventional residences, but they can potentially be just as costly. The size and cost of the land, how large the home will be, how the floor plan is set out, unique features to add to the home, and whether you're employing professionals or undertaking a DIY project are all factors to consider while building a house. When compared to a conventional house, you won't save much, if any, money if you want a large shipping container home with the finest amenities available. Minimizing your living requirements, on the other hand, may have a significant impact on your budget.

Your costs may vary significantly according to your requirements and the size of the shipping container house you want to construct. Financing choices may differ depending on how much money you'll need to complete your project. You may be able to use personal loans or credit cards to piece the project together. Construction loans for shipping container houses may be acquired for a bigger project, but banks may be reluctant to lend money to less well-known enterprises like shipping container homes. To offer yourself the greatest financial strength possible throughout the construction phase, maintain your credit score, save as much as you can, and avoid unnecessary expenditures. When your home payment is minimal or non-existent, being wise with your money now will pay you big time.

Always beware of bargains on goods, services, or equipment. Many costly instruments may be obtained at a fraction of the price at pawn shops, yard sales, or auctions. Look for shops that offer goods that are overstocked. Flooring, in particular, is often on sale at thrift and overstock shops. Most essential, make use of your relationships. If you know someone who works on homes, try if you can work out an arrangement with them to loan you equipment, perform labor for you at a reduced cost, or sell you surplus material. Friends who work in the construction business can also provide you with a lot of information and expertise. Rather of pestering them for information, try volunteering for them in your spare time in return for seeing what goes on at a building site. This may or might not work, but it's worth a go if you want to get some important experience.

Set Your Budget

While building a house, setting a budget is the first step. It's pointless to plan to construct a 4,000-square-foot house if you only have $50,000 to work with. Determine how much money you have in the bank. If you can borrow money from a bank or a family member, that amount will be in addition to the total amount of money you have available for the project. This is your financial plan.

Include a 20% contingency reserve in your budget. A contingency fund is an amount set aside to cover unforeseen costs that may arise during the development of your project. True, the bulk of construction projects involve unanticipated costs.

With total cash available of $150,000, this is how the contingency reserve is calculated. Calculate 20% of the total budget you have available, which in this case is $30,000. Subtract the $30,000 contingency payment from your $150,000 total available cash. This leaves you with the real budget for building your container house. Your construction budget is now $120,000, plus a $30,000 contingency budget. Your proposal must be built on the $120,000 figure, with $30,000 set aside for any problems that may occur.

2.2 Government and Local Code Considerations

You must prepare for the local authorities you will need to deal with depending on where you want to construct your shipping container house. These organizations will guarantee that your house is constructed to local code and that any required inspections are performed on schedule. There isn't just one solution for determining which rules and regulations you may be subject to. Some counties in some states do not need inspections, while others require building permits and frequent inspections during the construction process.

Visiting your local government agency, such as a city hall or county clerk's office, is the best method to verify compliance with local regulatory authorities. Even if these requests are handled by a different office, they will be able to point you in the appropriate place. When you meet with the relevant authorities face to face, they may collect the information they need about your project, tell you what you need to know, and arrange any required inspections. Despite personal experiences, most local regulatory authorities aren't trying to be the bad guys. In their view, taking the initiative to counsel them on how to do the correct thing would make you seem good. Though it's not a guarantee, it'll almost always provide you extra leeway if anything goes wrong as the project progresses. If you're moving into a new neighborhood, this is a wonderful opportunity to learn about the neighborhood and network.

2.3 Sourcing Containers, Materials, and Equipment

Speaking of container homes, it's clear that you should start with the container since it's the center of everything, and the type of container most commonly used to build homes is the 20-foot one.

If you don't want to utilize a 20' shipping container, a 40' option is the next best thing. You may even combine several containers. Another advantage of shipping container homes is their low cost. You may get containers in a variety of sizes to fit your project's size and budget. Shipping containers can be of conventional or "high cube" height, as well as various lengths. The height of a conventional shipping container is approximately 8' 6", while the height variation of a high cube variant is approximately 1'.

You won't be able to buy a shipping container off the shelf at your local hardware shop, so you'll have to locate a place to buy one and arrange delivery. A 20' shipping container can usually be purchased for $2000-$10,000 online, depending on its age. Typically, delivery choices are provided for an extra fee. Trucks that transport containers are pretty frequent, so you should anticipate spending somewhere between $400 and $2000, depending on where you bought the container and where it will be delivered. The freight market affects these prices as well. In a congested freight market, containers will become scarce, and shipping costs will rise.

When choosing a container, it is critical that you either physically examine the container or get some kind of warranty from the vendor to verify that the container is in reasonable shape. Shipping containers are used to transport a wide range of goods, including hazardous chemicals. Check the flooring for chemical saturation, metal corrosion, or rotting in the wood, and read some of the markings on the interior and exterior of the container if you physically examine it. Reading the marks may sometimes give you a good idea of what was in the container. Shipping labels and packing lists are often left over and attached to the sides. Take a look at them and read them to see if there are any significant red flags.

Most shipping container retailers will be able to transport to your location and install your container on the ground. Before delivery, it will be critical to have your site ready and prepped. While it is very easy for them to place the container on the ground, you must figure out how to place it on the foundation. This will be easy if you choose a concrete slab foundation since they may place it right on the slab.

If you are going to build your home on blocks or above a basement, you'll need to figure out how to get the container from where it was dumped to the foundation. To pick up and transport the container, a local crane service, a big forklift, or even a large excavator may be required. To prevent making it heavier and needing bigger equipment to move it, it is critical to have it correctly positioned first before constructing anything inside. A 20-foot shipping container will weigh between 4500 and 5000 pounds.

It's generally not difficult to get the right equipment for your job. You may discover equipment vendors that rent out their equipment by searching the internet or checking around your neighborhood. You may hire a contractor to perform a portion of the job for you if you don't feel comfortable running a piece of equipment yourself. It's important to remember that employing a contractor will cost extra money. If you believe you can operate the equipment, renting may be a smart choice. If you have a heavy-duty vehicle and trailer, or if you know someone who does, you may be able to avoid paying delivery fees. Pay careful attention to the terms and conditions of any rental agreement, and if you have any concerns, ask them. Equipment rental businesses are infamous for tying you up in additional fees and costs for trivial items.

You may concentrate on where you want to purchase your supplies after you've found your container and equipment. Building supplies are sold by a number of large retail companies. These are advantageous since materials may be purchased in tiny amounts. Lumber yards, electrical supply houses, plumbing supply houses, brick and block factories, and interior design shops offer alternatives to retail chain stores. Each kind of company will often sell the proper tools for each material and, on occasion, will rent them to you to keep prices down. Each choice has its own set of benefits, so it's essential to look around and discover what's available in your region.

You'll need to plan how you'll get the supplies to your place, just as you'll need to plan how you'll get the equipment to your location. Shingles, for example, are extremely heavy, and if you want to install a shingled roof on your container, you'll need many packages.

To obtain the appropriate quantity with a pickup truck, you'd have to make many journeys back and forth. Look for any shipping alternatives available where you purchase your supplies. Delivery is sometimes included in the cost of the supplies. If delivery is not a possibility, look for local hauling companies or a truck rental company on the internet or via local contacts.

Remember the fundamentals to make the entire planning process easier. A plot of land, a container, and construction supplies are all required. Then you must consider the equipment and tools required for each stage. Finally, evaluate your ability level to see whether you can do each task alone or if you'll need to hire assistance. Keep your local regulatory authorities in mind, so you don't violate the law by mistake. Also, even if you believe you can handle it yourself, keep in mind that certain professions need authorized installation.

Electrical, plumbing, and heating, ventilation and air conditioning (HVAC) are the most common of these trades.

Portable power and bathroom facilities are two more planning concerns before you get started. While if you're working alone, it's usually easy to meet your bathroom needs, it's something to keep in mind. More significantly, a generator may be required in the early stages of construction before any electrical lines are installed.

2.4 Planning utilities installation

To ensure that correct utilities are performed at the appropriate times, the procedures outlined in this chapter must be completed in tandem with the foundation and container placement. Depending on the foundation type you select, you'll have different degrees of access to the containers' undersides. Your plans for the container in the future are equally important. If you want to relocate your container to a new location in the future, it may be necessary to run some of your utilities from within the container.

The two most important considerations for a 20' container on a slab or raft foundation are where the main water line enters the container and where the wastewater line exits. These lines typically come underground until they are right under the home when they will then travel straight up into the house from below to avoid freezing. When using a slab or raft foundation, knowing where your water fixtures will be and where to get the necessary lines through is critical.

To ensure to have everything finished on time, you should contact your local water company to have a water meter installed as well as a sewer connection. If you don't have access to sewer service, you'll need to pay a contractor to construct a septic system. You'll also need to have a well dug if you don't have access to municipal water. Keep in mind that, to avoid contamination, wells and septic systems must be spaced apart. These steps may seem daunting, but they are only a few phone calls away from getting service started. The experts will then take care of the rest.

These services may be expensive, with good drilling ranging from $5.000-$10.000 on average and septic installation costing about $2.000-$5.000. Municipal water and sewer hookups may be considerably less expensive, although they may cost pricier in certain regions. When it comes to the financial load of these services, it's hard to predict what situation you'll face.

After you've connected your water meter and septic or sewage lines, you may connect the rest of your pipes to your foundation. The lines are routed underground by excavating a trench for a slab or raft foundation. You'll bring the pipes flush with the slab surface after they're at the place you want them to come up through the floor. You'll be able to cut through the floor and connect an extension of the pipe to carry it up into the home once the container is in place. Your wastewater lines will be treated in the same way. It's important to remember that wastewater pipes must go downhill to the sewer or septic system.

It is considerably simpler to install your plumbing beneath the home and have the containers set before making holes in the floor if you utilize a different kind of foundation. Plumbing and other utilities may be routed beneath the home most easily via basement foundations. Work beneath your home may be made much simpler by using cinder blocks in your foundation to create a crawl space. Whatever choice you choose, you may expect different degrees of difficulty and effort vs reward. The example home uses a slab to make placing the container simpler, but it also made running utilities more complex. Basements are the most convenient for running utilities, but constructing the foundation and placing containers takes a lot more time, money, and equipment.

For a brief overview of water lines, know that they start from the city's main pipe or from a well dug by a contractor. A water meter will be installed from a city water main by the city or water municipality. The water line will continue under your home, where it will turn up and into the bottom of the house, from the water meter. A well works in the same way, but without the need for a water meter since you won't be paying for it.

To summarize, the septic or sewer system begins with either a sewer line or a septic tank built by someone else. A huge pipe designed to handle wastewater, including solid waste, goes under the house and emerges at the bottom. All of the house's drains and toilets will flow downhill via pipes that connect to this main pipe. Septic systems include almost a hundred feet or more of subterranean pipes, also known as lateral lines. They run from the septic tank to the house. While the solid waste decomposes in the septic tank, these pipes enable treated wastewater to flow back into the earth.

You'll need at least a drawing of your floor plan to simplify where your electrical wires, plumbing, and HVAC systems will go. You should have a plan for where everything will go before you start putting up any walls or fixtures so you can identify any possible issues. Wiring, plumbing, and air ducts may be difficult to route in a shipping container house. As a result, it's essential to know where your water heater, furnace, bathroom, washing machines, and kitchen appliances will all go.

Electrical Lines

You may contact your local electric municipality to set up a new service to your house once your containers are in place. They will install utility poles, run extra lines, and put up a pedestal outside your house to mount your main breaker box and electric meter, among other things. You or a qualified electrician will run electricity to a breaker box within your house from this main breaker box. This box will distribute all circuits throughout your house. A local code enforcer may examine the installation of breaker boxes and electrical work in general. If you don’t trust on your ability to wire your house, it is better to employ a professional, licensed electrician. Before the work is examined, you may be obliged by law to have an electrician sign off on it.

You don't have to hire an electrician right away once the electric municipality connects your main breaker box to the electricity grid. It's probably better to contact an electrician about how to continue, although an electrician will typically need to partly install walls before running wire to outlets, switches, and light fixtures.

The purpose of contacting an electrician early is to determine the best way to extend cables to your home's distant reaches. Wires may be routed beneath the house or in the attic area in conventional home buildings. The same issues you face with water and sewage connections will continue in your shipping container house. You could put them in the ceiling and lower your ceiling a little, run exposed conduit, or attempt to route cables beneath the container, which is the most challenging choice. When addressing flooring later in this book, an alternate floor construction will be described that may make running utilities beneath the floor while remaining within the container simpler.

Because every circumstance is different, there is no one-size-fits-all approach.

Whether you start physically running cables or not, you'll need to figure out how many outlets you'll need, where they'll go, and what type of lighting you'll need. Light fixtures need the use of switches. In addition, you'll need specific outlets or wiring in your kitchen for a refrigerator, microwave, range, dishwasher, trash disposal, and any additional cabinet lights. An outlet is required for your washing machine, and your dryer may need a higher voltage outlet. Make sure to include outside lighting in your planning. You'll need to know what you need to wire up in order to set up your circuits, whether you do it yourself or hire an electrician.

Plumbing

You may start designing and building your water lines that sprout from your main water line after you've decided where your sinks, showers, washing machines, dishwasher, and toilets will go. Cross-stitched polyethylene pipe, often known as 'pex pipe,' is the most prevalent kind of pipe used today. This kind of tubing is simple to deal with and resists freezing and breakage. It's even color-coded for hot and cold water in red and blue. Any big hardware shop should have everything you need to run a pex pipe.

Your water heater will usually be placed near your internal breaker box for your electricity, regardless of where you chose to install it. Although this isn't always the case, it's typical to have a shared utility room with a breaker box, water heater, washing and dryer area, and furnace. In anyway, you will need to install a water heater in your house. Installation is generally straightforward. Making sure a drip pan sits underneath the water heater and is appropriately permitted to flow out under the container is a special concern. Because containers may rust, it's critical to avoid any water leaks. Furthermore, water heaters may be a fire danger. When constructing your home's walls, be sure there are no exposed wood studs near the water heater.

You may run the pex lines and cap them off temporarily while you juggle constructing walls, installing cabinets, and other features until you're ready to install sinks or other water fixtures are needed. This will enable you to get things up and running before committing to a permanent solution. As you construct, be careful not to block off access to specific lines. This is particularly essential when it comes to wastewater pipes. Keep in mind the location of your toilets and drains in relation to your sewage line, as well as how you'll connect them.

Natural Gas Systems

Though often considered a luxury, natural gas systems can be an efficient way to heat your home and offer you the benefit of a gas range. Even if you build your shipping container home in a remote area, natural gas companies can set you up with your own natural gas tank that sits outside your home. From there, a licensed technician can run gas lines into your shipping container home to run your water heater, furnace, and range.

Having natural gas in your home is often a nice feature, but you will want to be cautious of a few things. Never tamper with any components of your system. Gas explosions can completely destroy a home. When used correctly, you have little to no risk of anything going wrong. However, it's worth mentioning that some people don't know their limits when trying to work in their own homes.

A more common and realistic concern, however, is the presence of carbon monoxide. If you burn anything in your home, from natural gas to candles, you will have very small quantities of carbon monoxide in your home. Carbon monoxide is a colorless, odorless gas that is potentially lethal to humans. Carbon monoxide detectors can be purchased and work very similarly to smoke alarms. Even better with today's technology, carbon monoxide detectors, smoke alarms, thermostats, and security systems can all be combined and controlled via smartphone.

For a shipping container home, these detectors are all critically important since you are living in a smaller space. If your home has carbon monoxide present or if a fire breaks out, you may only have one way out and nearly no time to get there. If you have children or own pets, monitoring these systems can give you the peace of mind and security you need to happily live your life. These high-tech systems can also save you money on utilities and insurance costs.

Don't let carbon monoxide scare you from a natural gas system. Natural gas systems are very nice to have if you choose to install one. It is simply something that everyone should know in the extremely unlikely event something bad were to happen.

HVAC (Heating, Ventilation, and Air Conditioning)

Steel is used to construct shipping container houses. Steel is a great conductor of heat. As a result, your container will want to get very hot in the summer and extremely chilly in the winter. When we talk about wall construction, we'll talk about insulation types and how to install them, but for now, we'll talk about how to install your heater, air conditioner, and ventilation system. The heater and fan system for a central air system are usually placed alongside the water heater and panel box in a utility room, as previously mentioned. You may go with a basic window unit and space heater for a tiny 20' shipping container. We will, however, discuss a central heating and cooling system.

It is generally better to leave the installation of an HVAC system to a professional. These systems are very complicated, with many equipment warranties and a slew of rules governing how to manage the refrigerant used in air conditioning. There is a lot of electrical work involved, and since HVAC repairs may be expensive, it's generally better to get it done the first time properly.

The ventilation component is considerably simpler for a do-it-yourself builder. A popular technique for heating and cooling a shipping container house is to install an air duct down the length of the container from one of the top corners. This duct may either be perforated to enable air to gently seep out and disperse around the house, or it can be covered with drywall and trim and vented via metal vents, as in conventional houses. It all boils down to personal taste.

Once your ductwork is finished, double-check that your home's air conditioner breathes air out the top. It's simple to connect it to your

ductwork, but be sure to follow the manufacturer's instructions to prevent voiding your warranty. Because HVAC systems are infamous for breaking down, keeping your warranty current is essential to save money in the long run.

It should be better that your outdoor air conditioning equipment could be installed by a professional. The copper pipe and electrical connections must be run correctly for the system to work effectively. A professional will also have the necessary equipment to properly charge and maintain your system. Finally, if you want a certain kind of thermostat system, choose one ahead of time and show it to the expert who will be installing it. Many contemporary thermostats may connect to your phone, security system, or other home automation device. They may assist you with lowering your energy expenses and extending the life of your system.

Installing your HVAC system, like all other stages in this procedure, may need some tip-toeing around other ongoing processes. Keep in mind how your walls are built, where your electrical lines are already routed, and all that may get in the way of your ductwork. The majority of utility work is doing extensive research to determine who the finest experts in your region are and then employing them. Maintain contact with them to verify that you receive what you want and that they are capable of doing well.

2.5 Designing your home

So, after you've considered your requirements and done your research on local laws, it's time to start building your house. This is where you can actually let your imagination run wild. A single container house is the most basic design, and you may go as far as you want with it. Two-story? Three? The options are limitless, and they may be tailored to meet your specific requirements.

Most people stick to single-story houses, others stack containers until they reach the required size. Interior walls may be installed to divide a container into several rooms, and connecting walls can be removed to expand the floor area of a room. The bedroom, living room, kitchen, bathroom, and pantry are the essentials, and all of these may be crammed into a single 20-foot container provided you're okay with a small living area.

A simple internet search will turn up a plethora of free software packages to assist you in designing your shipping container house. If you are not comfortable doing it on your own, an architect's fee should be included in your budget. Typically, bids for such a tiny living area will not be outrageous. However, try it and see what happens. Designing your home will likely be easier than you think, and being in charge of the process can be quite fun.

Sample Plans

These are just a few floor plans that show the customization potential of container homes. Take a look and get inspired.

Floor plan 1 - 1 container

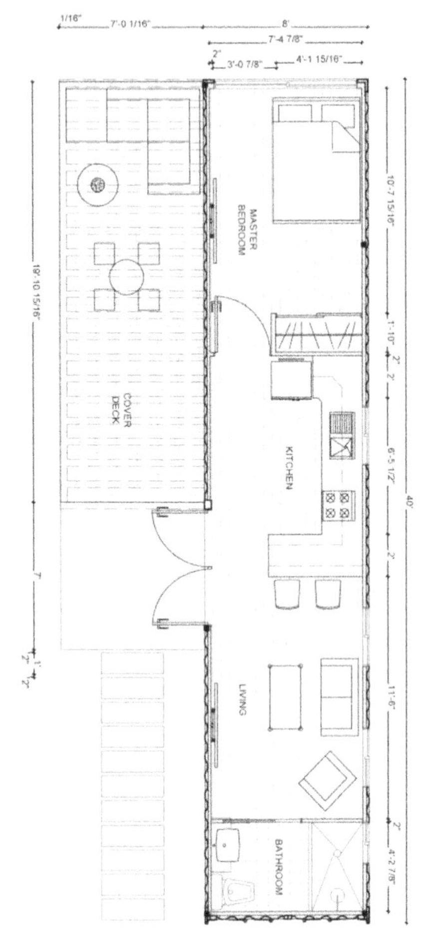

This Shipping Container Home was proposed with a 40ft. Shipping Container High Cube, with a cover deck next to the house, so the people can enjoy a coffee at afternoon. Has a master bedroom with a small closet, one bathroom with shower and a common area with open space concept where are the kitchen, living and a small breakfast table.

Floor plan 2 - 1 container

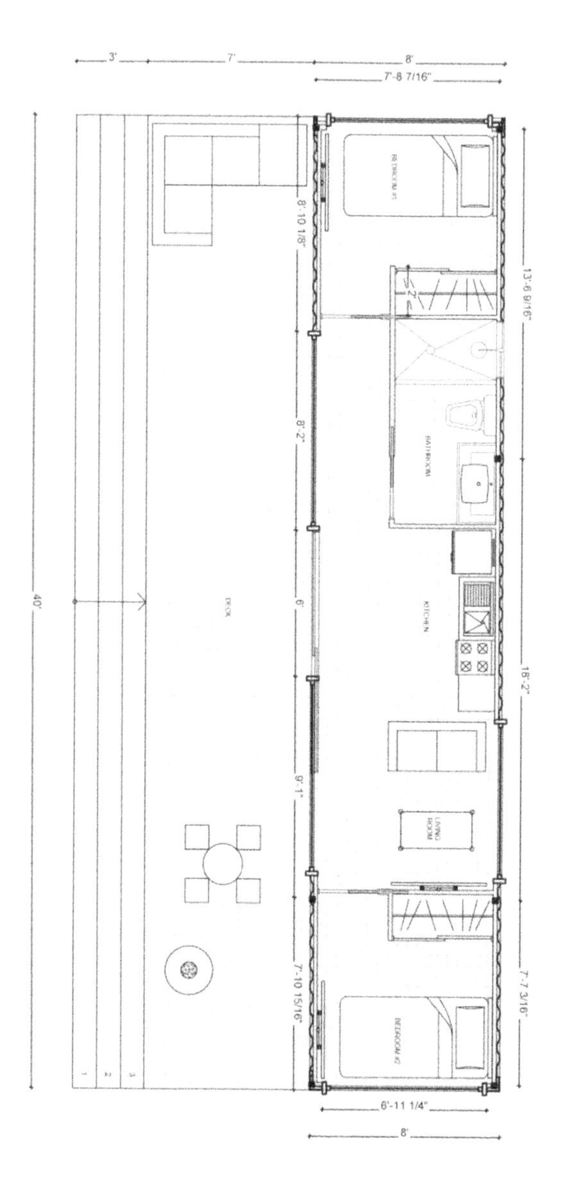

This project was designed like a student apartment with one 40ft. Shipping Container, with two small bedrooms and one bathroom for both bedrooms. Also has a little kitchen and living room with TV wall. Outdoor has a deck to enjoy a bbq with the friends.

Floor plan 3 - 1 container

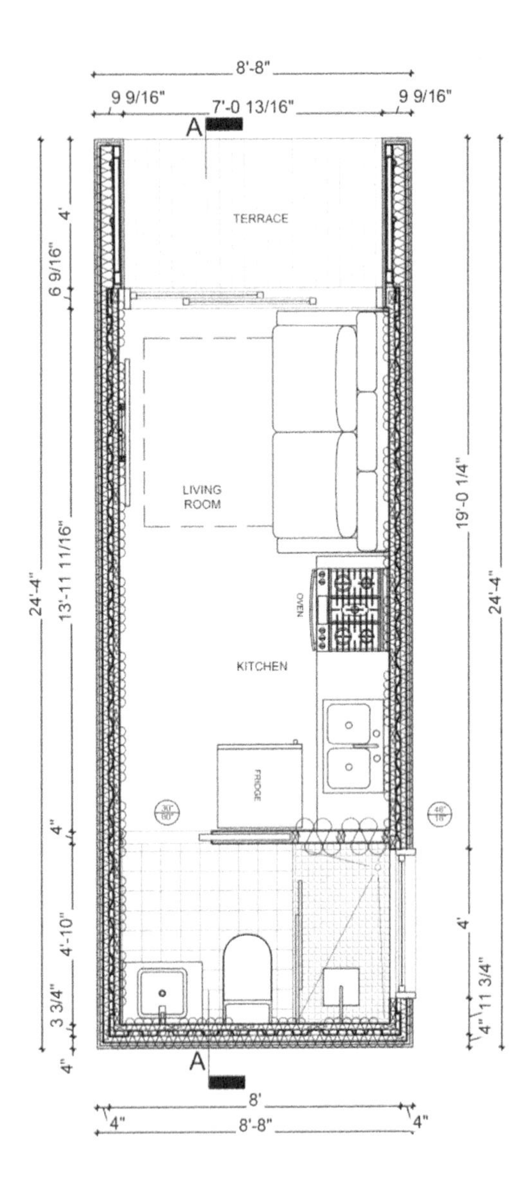

This project was created with a single 20ft shipping container, could be used at backyard house like an ADU or guest room. Has a comfortable bathroom, kitchen and a space with a coach/bed. Also, a little terrace.

Floor plan 4 - 1 container

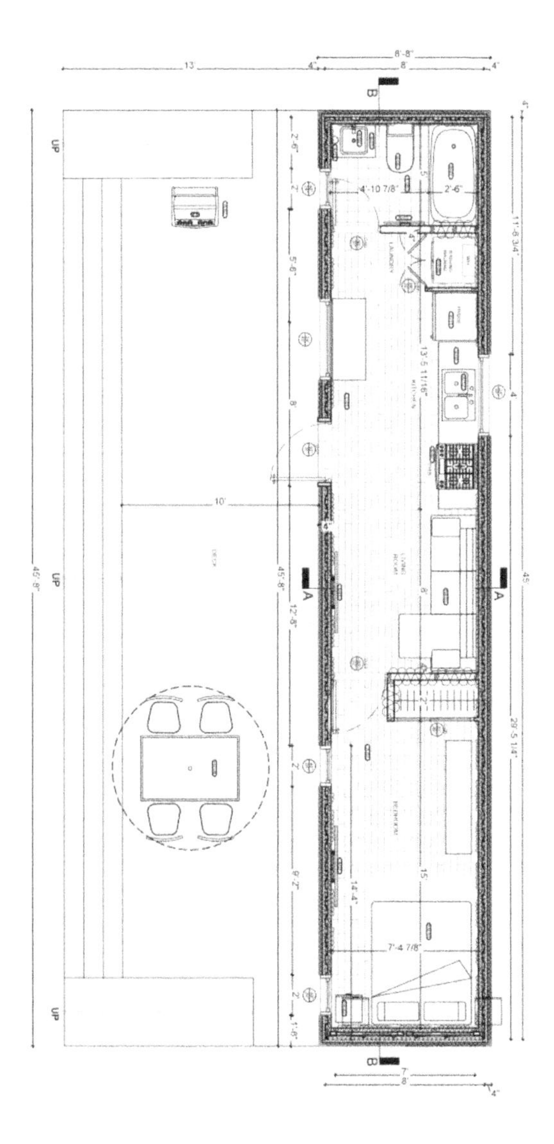

This project was designed with one 40ft. Shipping container High Cube. Has a comfortable bedroom with closet, also, has a great open space concept of common area with kitchen, laundry and living room with a small breakfast table. A bathroom with bathtub always is important in any project and of course, an outdoor deck to share with family and friend of a great BBQ.

Floor plan 5 - 2 containers

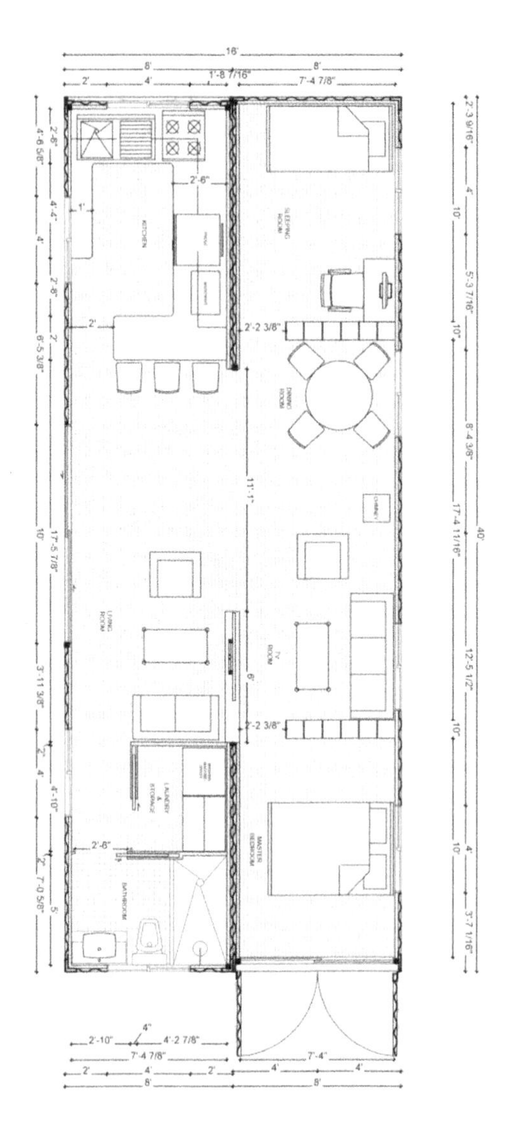

This project was designed with two 40ft. Shipping Containers High Cube joined side by side. Whole interior space is with open concept. Bedroom are separated by shelfs with the common area and has a small kitchen and one bathroom for whole house.

Floor plan 6 - 2 containers

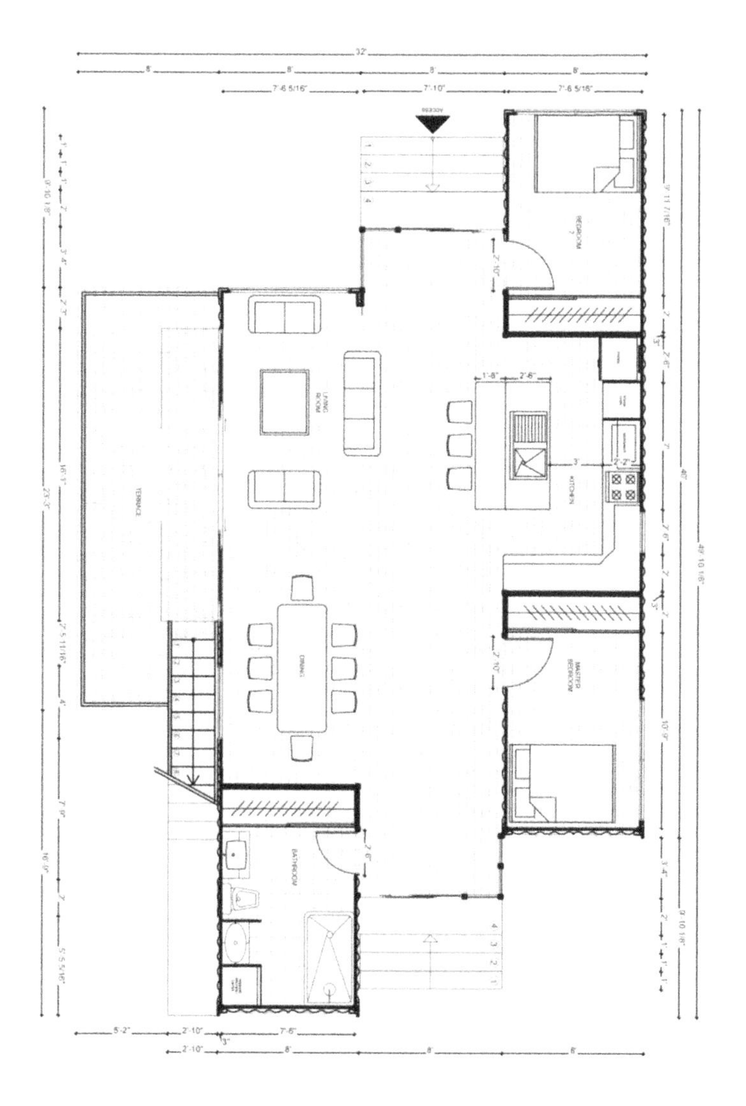

This project was created with two 40ft. shipping containers spaced 8' between them to do the interior rooms bigger. Has 2 bedrooms with closets, a kitchen with island and the living and dining room front to the deck, so there could enjoy a great view. Also, from the deck you can go to the rooftop above the first container.

Floor plan 7 - 2 containers

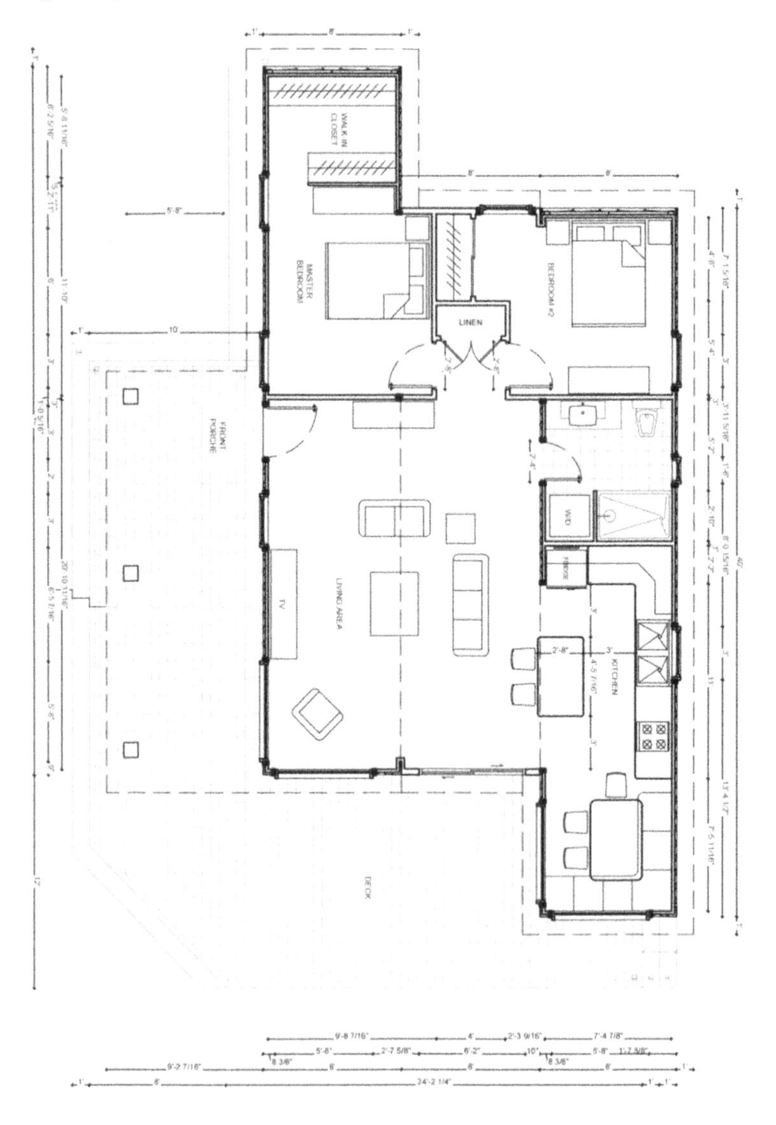

This project was proposed with two 40ft. shipping containers spaced 8' between them, with a deck around them with a cover area and another one uncovered. Has two bedrooms, one is a master bedroom with a walk-in closet and the other one has a closet. A common area with a comfortable kitchen and dining table and a big living room. One bathroom that includes a laundry closet

Floor plan 8 - 2 containers

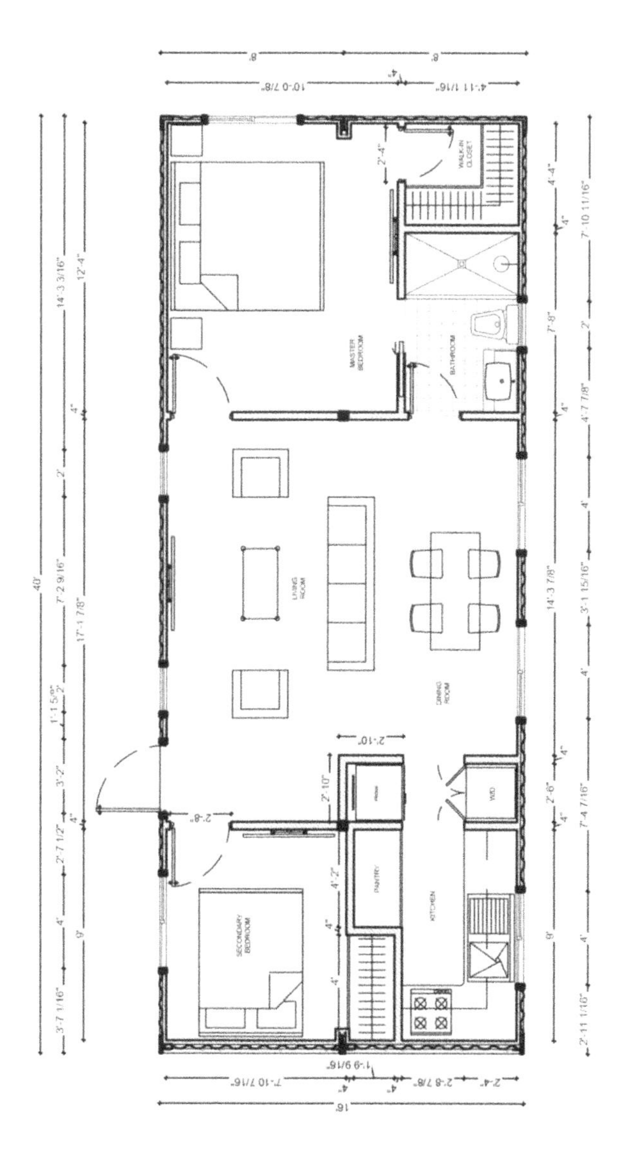

This project was designed with two 40ft. Shipping containers with one comfortable master bedroom with a walk-in closet and a shared bathroom with the common area. Also has a secondary bedroom and a small kitchen that includes a laundry closet.

Floor plan 9 - 2 containers

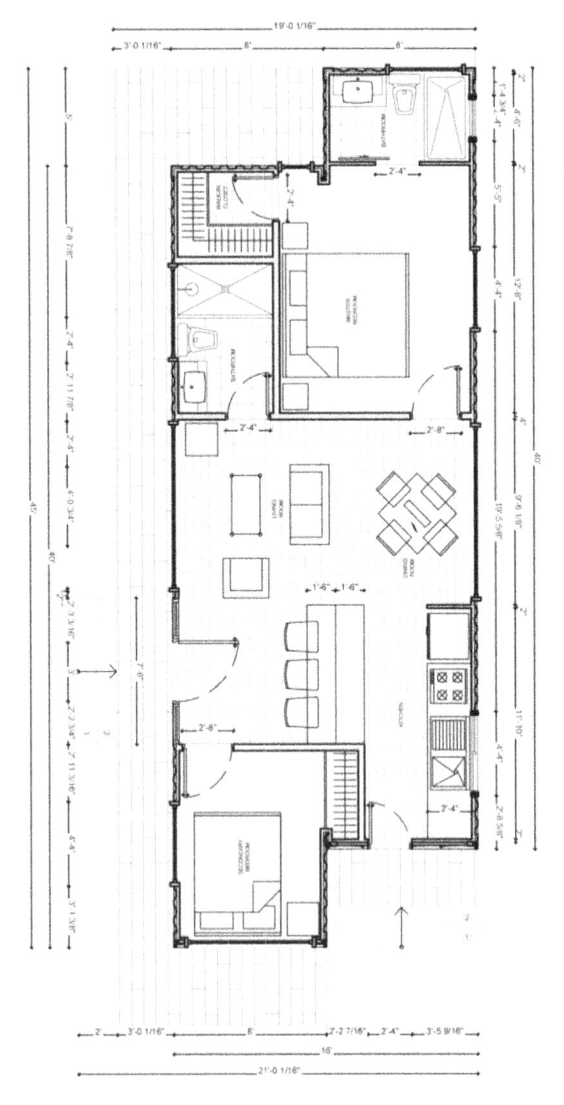

This project was proposed with two 40ft. shipping containers joined and displacements 5' one each another. Has a common area with open space concept with a living, dining and kitchen room. Kitchen has a breakfast table for 3 persons. In the private rooms has two bedrooms, a master bedroom with private bathroom and a walk-in closet. Another bedroom is secondary, and share the bathroom with the common area.

Floor plan 10 - 3 containers

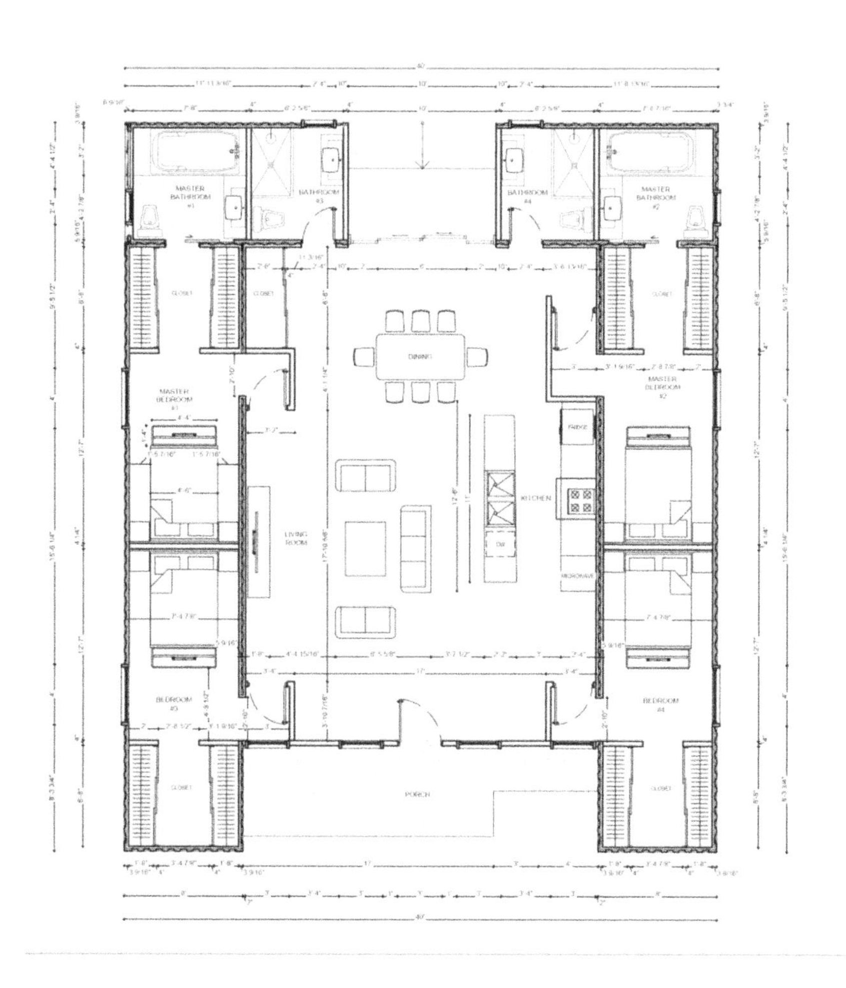

This project was designed with three 40ft. shipping containers placed like a “U” shape. Between them, a comfortable open space concept of living room, dining room and kitchen with island. Four small bedrooms, all of these with walk-in closet but two of them with a private bathroom, and two bathrooms more for the rest of the house

Floor plan 11 - 3 containers

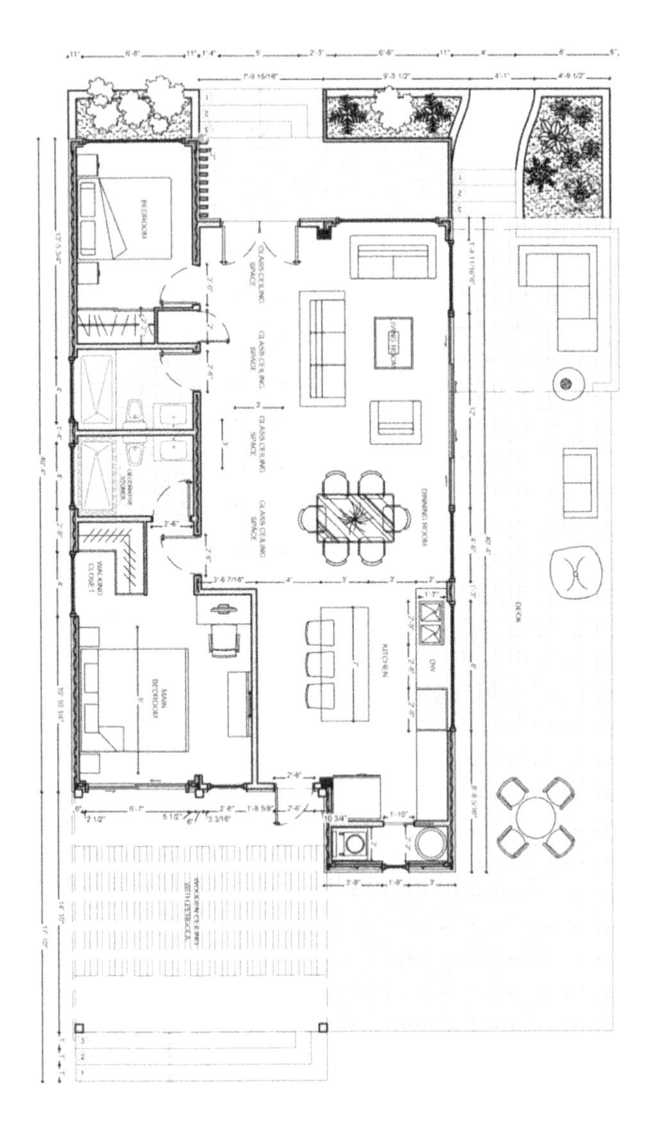

This project was designed like a comfortable house, with three 40ft. shipping containers and a deck around them, with a covered area with pergolas like a modern concept. Indoor a modern open space with the living, dining and kitchen. Also two bedrooms, one a master bedroom with private bathroom and the other one with shared bathroom with the common area.

Floor plan 12 – 2 storey

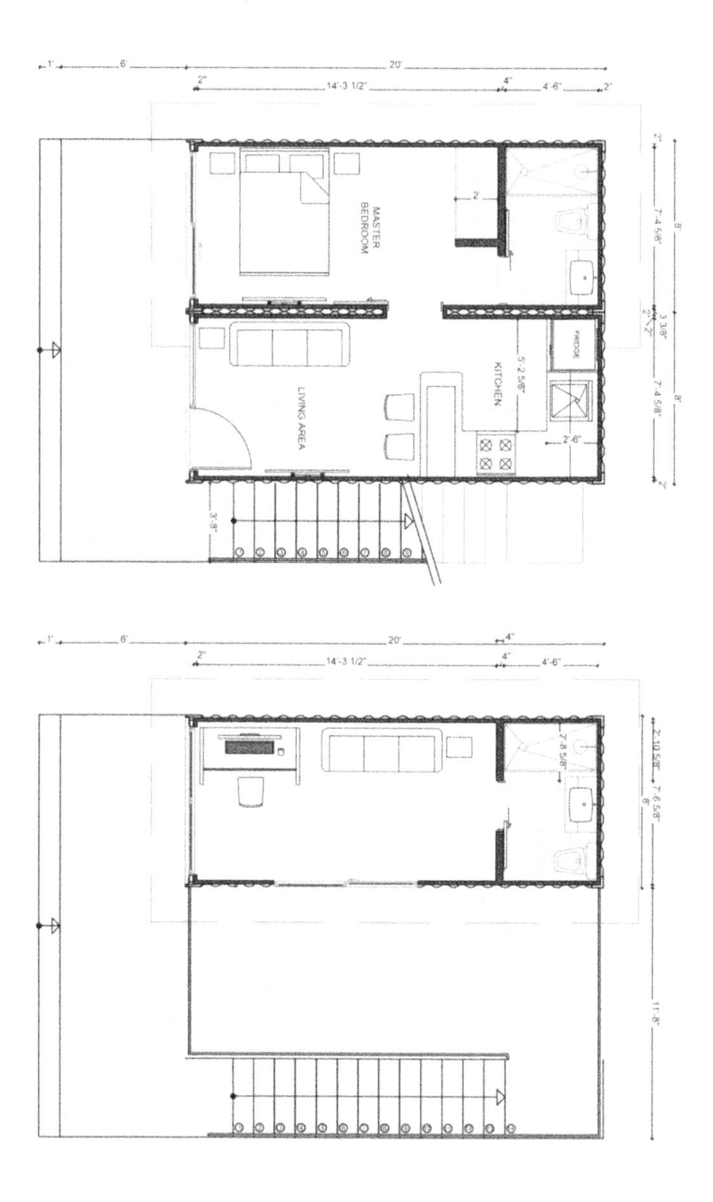

This project was designed like a home with exterior office above it. Designed with three 20ft. Shipping Containers. On ground floor are two of them, where are a master bedroom and a kitchen/living room, and on second floor with a terrace, an office to work and receives customers.

Floor plan 13 – 2 storey

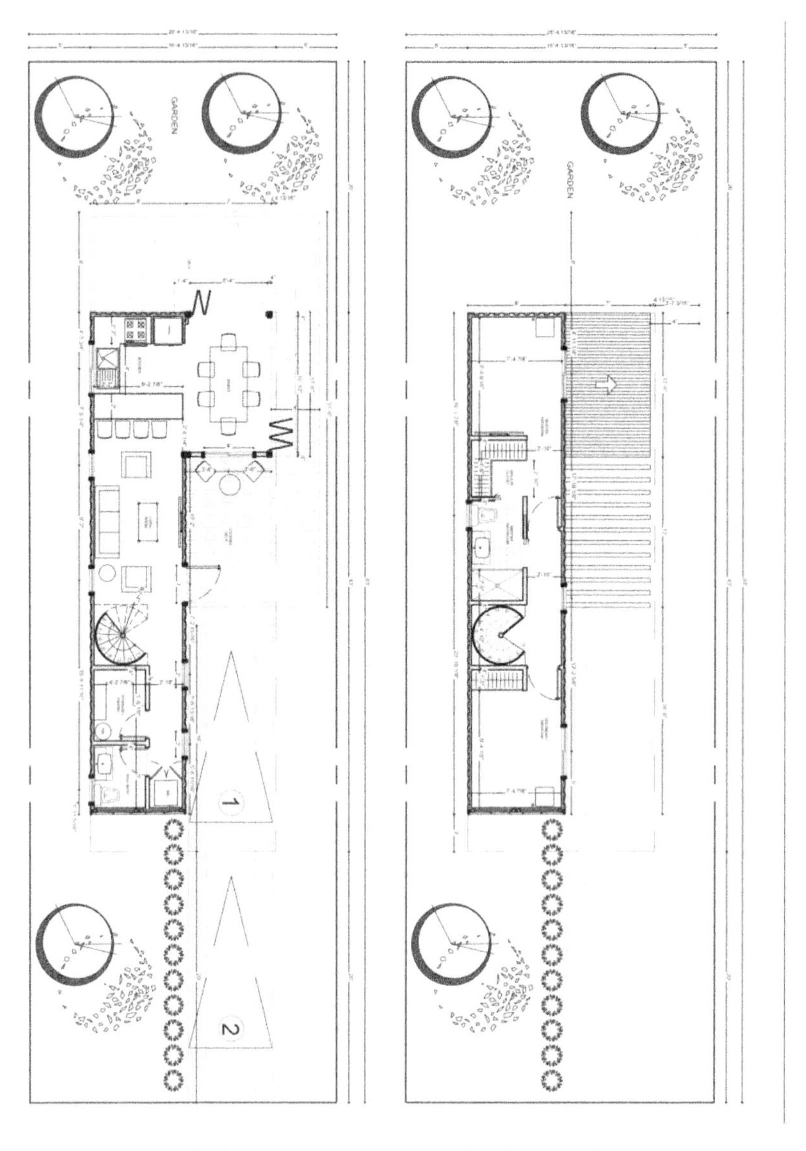

This project was designed with two stacked 40ft. shipping containers, a house with two bedrooms on the second floor and on the ground floor a comfortable common area. On back side of the house, a deck to enjoy the backyard and at front side a covered porch before to enter to the house.

Floor plan 14 – Luxury

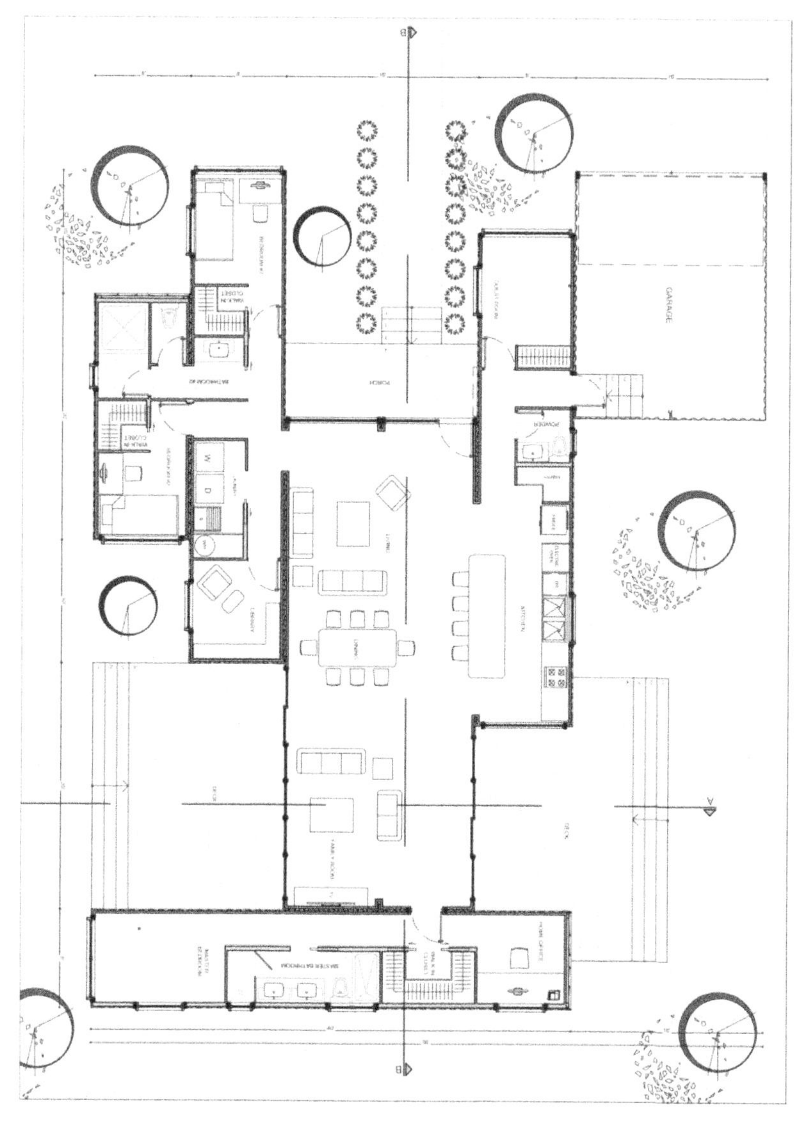

This project was projected like a luxury house with three 40ft. and three 20ft. shipping containers. At center them, was spaced to create the common area with the living room, dining room and a family room with a high ceiling. Common area works like a meeting point where at south has two small bedrooms, laundry room, bathroom and a library. To East the master bedroom inside of a

40ft. shipping container with a private office, a walk-in closet, a comfortable master bathroom with two sinks and one shower and bathtub. To North side, a guestroom with bathroom and the kitchen. Also at North side is a garage with two cars spots inside of two 20ft. shipping containers joined.

Floor plan 15– Luxury

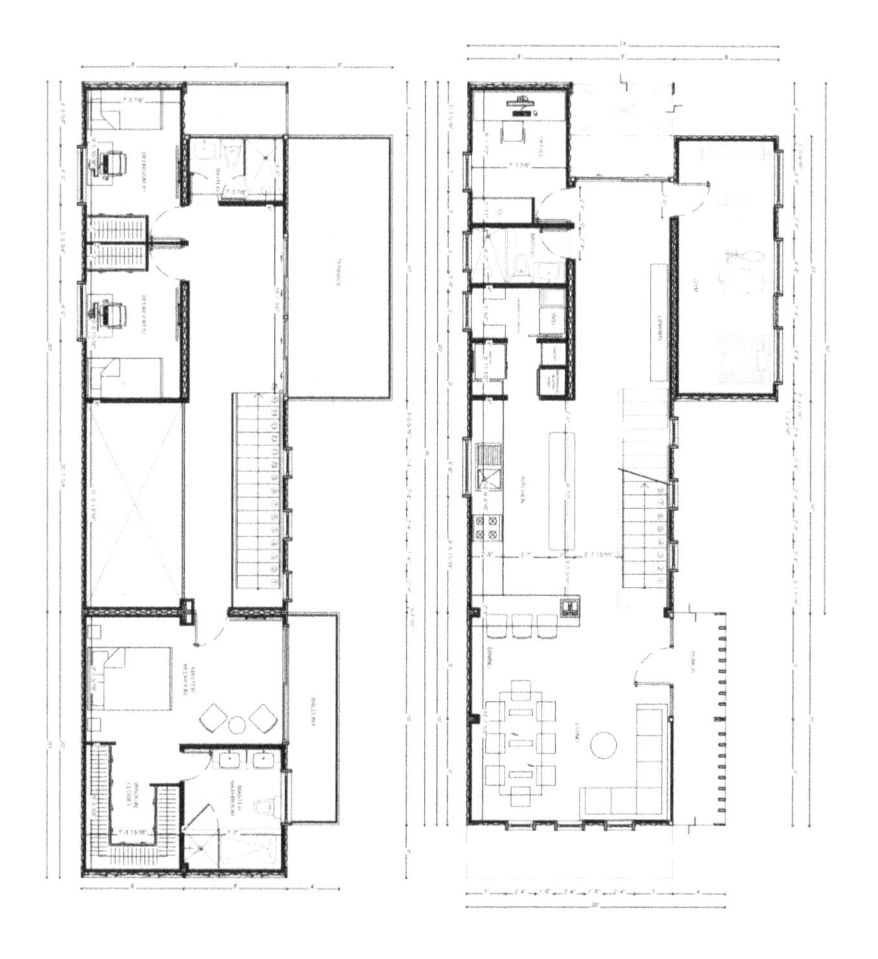

This project was designed like a luxury 2 stories house with shipping containers. Four containers stacked on another four containers, two 40ft and two 20ft shipping containers and another one on ground floor of 20ft. where is the Gym room.

On ground floor, a comfortable living and dining room, a kitchen and a complete laundry and pantry room. Also, an office and a private gym with a bathroom.

On second floor, two secondary bedrooms with a shared bathroom and the master bedroom with a comfortable master bathroom and a walk-in closet and a private balcony. On second floor common area, has a terrace above the gym.

Planning Checklist

- Plan out the needs of your home. Set your budget.
- Meet with the local planning authorities to find the specifications and required paperwork for your area.
- Design your home.
- Obtain planning permission, if necessary.

Chapter 3
Choosing the Containers

There are a variety of sourcing possibilities, so here is some information to help you familiarize yourself with the options and navigate the purchase. First, let's have a look at the container dimensions.

The 20-foot and 40-foot containers, both of which are available in normal and high cube sizes, will be the most popular choices. High cube containers provide an extra foot of height to your container, which may be useful if you intend to build a ceiling in your house. The interior and exterior dimensions of each of these choices are shown in the tables below:

External Dimensions

	Length	Width	Height
Standard 20 Foot	19'10 1/2" (6.06m)	8' (2.44m)	8'6" (2.59m)
Standard 40 Foot	40' (12.19m)	8' (2.44m)	8'6"(2.59m)
High Cube 20 Foot	19'10 1/2" (6.06m)	8' (2.44m)	9'6" (2.90m)
High Cube 40 Foot	40' (12.19m)	8' (2.44m)	9'6" (2.90m)

Internal Dimensions

	Length	Width	Height
Standard 20 Foot	19' 4 (5.89m)	7' 8 (2.34m)	7'10 (2.39m)
Standard 40 Foot	39' 5 (12.01m)	7' 8 (2.34m)	7'10 (2.39m)
High Cube 20 Foot	19' 4 (5.89m)	7' 8 (2.34m)	8'10 (2.69m)
High Cube 40 Foot	39' 5 (12.01m)	7' 8 (2.34m)	8'10 (2.69m)

Your best choices will be determined by the designs you've drawn up as well as the availability of containers in your region, since transportation charges may be very expensive if you buy a container from a location far away from where you want to construct. Also, bear in mind that each manufacturer has its own tolerance level for dimensioning, so it's better to get all of your containers from the same company.

3.1 New or Used?

One of the things you have to choose first while looking for containers is whether you want to buy new ones or no. You also have a third choice. One-trip containers are available for purchase. They are used to transport goods to their destination and then sold after the cargo has been delivered. This is a great choice if you can locate one-trip containers that meet your requirements. They will be far less expensive than new containers since they will not have the wear and tear that is common in used containers.

New and one-trip containers are the simplest to deal with, and they're usually in better shape. There will be no rust, mold, or unidentified chemical contamination. It is simpler to construct using them, and they have a longer lifespan.

Because used containers are often exposed to pesticides or lead-based paints, you may need to take an extra step in constructing your house and making it habitable. If you're on a strict budget, however, you may certainly save money by purchasing old containers. If your choice is to buy a used container, here are some things to check for before making a purchase:

Leaks

This is a significant issue. You don't want a leaky house, and holes that let water in also let other annoyances in. Make that the container's roof and walls are in good working order. Also, sniff the container's inside to check whether there's a trace of mold. Another sign of potential leakage is this.

Rust

When buying a second-hand container, you can anticipate some minor rusting. However, if the rusting has gotten to the point where the metal's integrity is being jeopardized, you should look for another container. When doing your examination, remember to look at the roof as well.

Functional Doors and Locks

Check the doors to verify that they swing freely and that the seal is intact, then bolt them to ensure that they latch firmly.

Wooden Flooring in Good Repair

When a container is in use, it's normal for it to become a little battered. However, you should examine the hardwood flooring to ensure that it is free of holes and breaks. If you inadvertently buy a container with damaged flooring, the original flooring may be covered with a non-permeable layer and utilized as is, resulting in an extra, time-consuming stage in the building.

Chemical Contamination

This is when your sense of smell will come in useful. You're looking for something out of the ordinary to scent. When used, containers may be exposed to pesticides or other chemical dangers. When buying a container, inquire about its history, but conduct your own research to ensure you aren't exposing yourself or your family to toxins.

Intact Identification Code

The shipping container identification code is an 11-digit alphanumeric code inscribed into the container. The history of a container can be tracked with this code, meaning that you can use it to see where it has been and what it has carried.

Here is a sample Identification code:

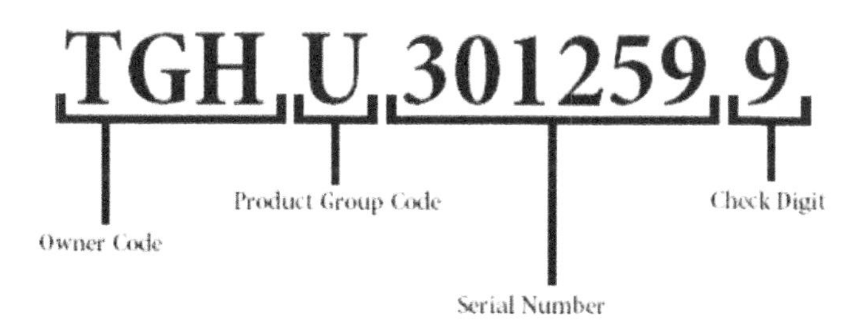

The first three digits, the owner code, identify the owner of the container. The fourth digit, the product group code, is a single letter.

The only options for this digit are J, U, and Z. J indicates that there is equipment attached, while Z indicates a container trailer. If you are looking at a standard shipping container, you will see a U in this position. The remainder of the code is devoted to a six-digit serial number which indicates the precise container, and a single number used as a check digit to verify the authenticity of the code. You can use this code to verify information about the container's history.

3.2 Where Can you Purchase It?

Shipping containers can be purchased from many sources. They are available in surplus all over the world. What you want to look for is a reputable dealer.

These can be found easily with a Google search. Just search for "shipping container dealer" and add your location. This will yield a number of dealers in your area.

Alternately, you can type "buy shipping container in ..." and add your location. The search results should be similar, if not identical.

One tool which helps those in search of shipping containers is the Green Cube Network. This is a search tool that helps to find shipping containers in your area.

It's great for homing in on a list of dealers. Here is a link that will bring you straight to their search tool:

http://www.greencubenetwork.org/shipping-container-dealers_3/

If you're still having trouble, try out Alibaba, eBay, or Gumtree.

Container Purchasing Checklist

- Determine your budget for containers.
- Make any design adjustments necessary, factoring in the price of available containers.
- Decide on new, used, or one-time use containers.
- Source the containers from a reliable local supplier.
- If possible, inspect the container before purchase.

Chapter 4

How to Build Your Container Home: Step-By-Step Procedure, Techniques and Tips

Now that we've explained how to choose your container, it's time to talk about operational steps, from site preparation to the actual construction of your container home

Other important considerations include the budget for shipping new, used, or one-time use containers and the location from which they are being shipped. We'll take all of these considerations in turn with the sections that follow.

4.1 Site Preparation and Soil Types

The first stage in site preparation is to determine the soil type. You should choose the foundation that is most suitable for your site. There are a few choices here, and which one you pick will be determined by the soil composition of your construction site.

Concrete piers, raft foundations, trench footings, and piles are the most typical foundations for shipping container houses. To figure out which is ideal for you, you'll need to understand the qualities of each and the soil in your area. Some people like to "over-spec" their foundations, making them strong enough to resist pressures greater than the structure would ever need. After you've considered all of your choices, it's ultimately up to you.

Soil Types

I mean, isn't dirt simply dirt? Wrong. There are many soil kinds, each of which may support a distinct structural load. Here's a rundown of the many soil types you may come across on your construction site, as well as some of the construction considerations that go along with them:

Rock

It's really a blessing if your construction site is a slab of rock. To construct on top of this, you just need to make sure it's level and remove the surface dirt. Granite, schist, or diabase are examples of this kind of rock. It has a large load-bearing capability and can support anything you put on it. Concrete pier foundations are one of the cheapest and simplest foundations to utilize in these circumstances.

Gravel

We've probably all heard of gravel. It's a coarse-grained substance that's easy to dig up and drains well. Trench footing is the finest foundation for this kind of soil.

Clay

Clay has a very fine grain and can retain a lot of water. If your construction site is a clay-based soil, you may be in for some expensive preparation. You'll have to dig deeper until you come upon more solid dirt. The best foundations for this soil type are pile foundations or deep trench footings.

Sandy Soil

Sand is made up of fine-grained particles that are often mixed with gravel and rock. It's crucial not to over-dig the foundation while dealing with these soils. This may put more strain on the softer soils under the sand layer. The raft foundation, also known as a slab-on-grade, is the ideal foundation for this soil type.

What Soil Type Do I Have?

Unless you're a geotechnical engineer or the soil type is very apparent, you should seek expert assistance at this point. The geotechnical engineer will conduct a thorough investigation of the whole site, including soil borings, to determine the soil composition at various depths. This will make you better understand what you're dealing with and the finest foundation for supporting your home.

A soil engineer would typically drill test bores every 100 to 150 feet throughout the site. These test bearings will provide a soil profile, indicating the load-bearing capacity of the soil. These tests will reveal the soil's water content, density, and particle size, as well as its categorization, depth of various soil kinds, and groundwater level. Bores will be extended for at least another 20 feet into load-bearing earth.

Geotechnical engineers will also investigate the surface characteristics of the soil, looking for soils that provide a problem to the construction process. They'll look at the site's elevation and provide suggestions for how it may be leveled most efficiently. Essentially, the geotechnical engineer will provide a report that states:

- Soil type on the surface
- Soil type under the surface
- Bearing capacity of the soil
- The depth of the groundwater
- The depth of the frost
- Compaction of the soil
- Type of foundation to use
- Minimum foundation depth
- Sufficient drainage

Tip: Sometimes, the local authority has information on the soil profile of your area. If you plan to build within city limits, this

is a high likelihood. If you are building something a bit further out, you can almost guarantee that a soil profile will be necessary and should factor this into your budget.

4.2 Foundations: Which Ones Are Best Suited to Your Soil Type and How to Build Them

We've already explored the four foundation types that you will need to know about when preparing your site. They are concrete piers, raft foundations, trench footings, and pile foundations.

Here are a few structural and geotechnical details about each foundation to help you select the one right for your shipping container home. Also included are all the details you'll need to plan and lay the foundation of your home.

This being said, it's important to meet with a structural engineer to make sure that your foundation can hold the necessary load and that it's designed to the specifications you need.

Concrete Piers

Essentially, concrete piers are steel-reinforced concrete cubes laid out at the corners and load-bearing center of your structure. For a single container, you will need six of these cubes, one at each corner and two to support the outer walls at the center of your structure.

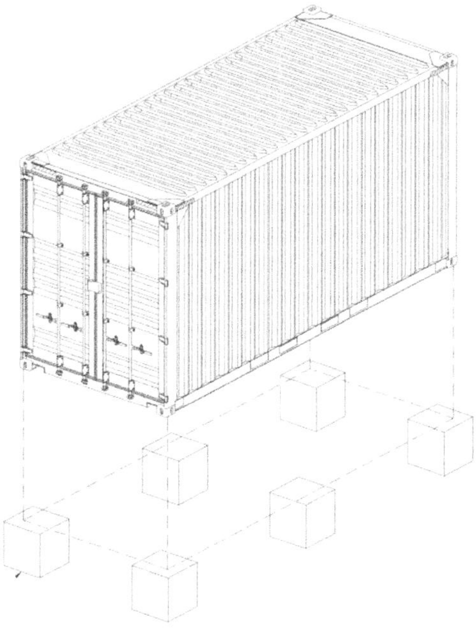

They offer a shallow foundation and are both cheap and DIY-friendly. Additional benefits include the fact that the container will be elevated off the soil with this foundation type, reducing the need for insulation, allowing ventilation, and reducing the build-up of condensation on the floor of the container. Below is a diagram that indicates the placement of the piers:

Laying Your Concrete Pier Foundation

The first step in laying your foundation is to determine the placement of the corners. This is a set of instructions that offers step-by-step details on how to plot out and lay the foundation for a 40-ft. container.

1. Begin with one corner and drive a 2 in. x 2 in. 1-ft. stake 6 in. into the ground.

2. Nail a 40-ft. string into the top of the first stake, and then use this first stake as a marker to measure 40 ft. to the second corner. Nail a second stake into the ground, just as you have done the first.

   You have now marked out the length of your container.

3. Attach a 40-ft., 9.5 in. string to one stake and another 8-ft. string to the other.
4. Ensuring that both strings are taut, find their intersection point. This is the third corner of your container. Nail another stake into this point.

5. Repeat step three to determine the final corner of your container.

6. Run a line between two of the corners of your container, lengthwise.

7. Use a tape measure to determine the point 20 ft. along this line from one corner.

8. Repeat step 6 to find the point along the length of your container on the other side.

9. Once you have marked out the placement of the piers, dig a hole 50cm deep, 50cm wide, and 50cm long (50cm is about 2 ft., 4 in.).

10. Place a form around the hole. You may choose to use pre-made concrete forms at this time. Sonotubes© work extremely well for this purpose. If you are creating the form on your own, 1.5 mm, the plastic lining will do the trick.

11. Once you have placed the form, line the space of the pier with rebar in a grid formation. Try to ensure that you place three across the length and three across the width, binding the rebar together with steel wire. Repeat this pattern vertically every 6 in.

12. Drive three reinforced metal bars through the foot of the pier vertically, using these to stabilize each horizontal level of rebar reinforcement. Tie each horizontal level into these bars.

13. Fill these holes with concrete.

14. Before placing it, the concrete has to cure for at least seven days before placement. (More details on curing concrete and selecting the appropriate concrete for your foundation can be found below.)

Offered below are a few diagrams which illustrate the measuring and laying of the concrete pier foundation.

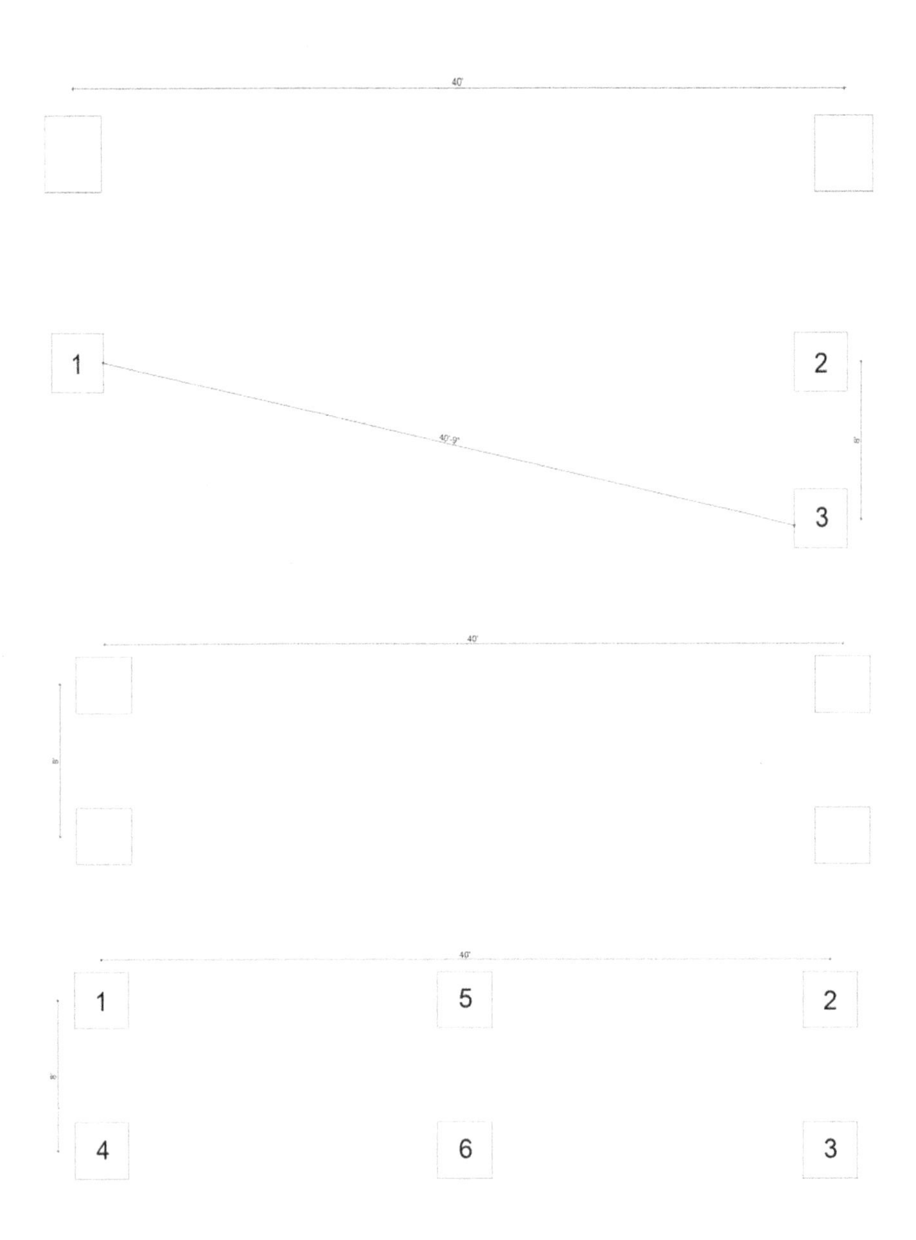

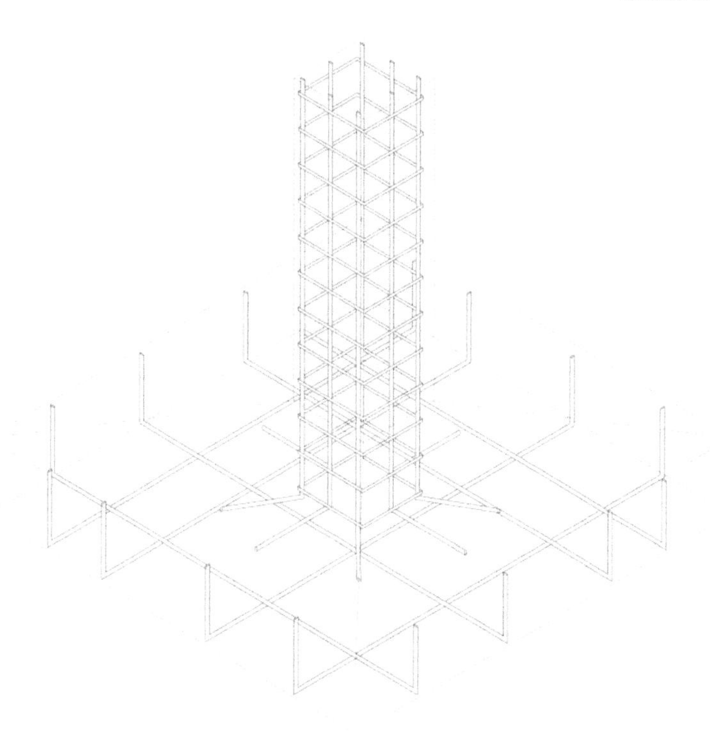

Piling Foundation

Essentially, pile foundations are exactly the same as pier foundations. The only difference is that they are driven deeper into the ground. They are best for moving past unsuitable soils and driving into a soil type more capable of bearing a load. The measurement is the same; however, in order to drive the piles, you will likely need specialized equipment. Therefore, this is one of the most expensive options.

Piles are cylindrical steel tubes that are driven into the ground until they reach a suitable soil depth. Once the piles reach a soil capable of bearing a load, they are filled with concrete.

Above ground, a pile foundation looks very similar to a pier foundation. To lay a pile foundation, you will need to contract a pile driver and purchase the cylinders to house the piles.

This makes it one of the less desirable foundation types for a DIY build. However, it can be an indispensable option when dealing with more troublesome soil types.

Raft Foundation

This foundation type is often known in the construction industry as slab-on-grade. Essentially, it involves leveling a space of ground, digging down to the required depth, and then placing a layer of concrete that will support the entire length and width of your structure.

The slab-on-grade is more costly in terms of time and resources than the trench foundation or concrete pier; however, it is ideal for sandy and loose soils. It essentially creates a structure that floats above unstable material, offering a solid foundation on loose soils without requiring you to dig down to a solid subgrade. When your soil type is unsuitable for a great depth, the slab-on-grade offers an elegant solution that does not require the heavy machinery costs of a pile driver.

Although the raft foundation is excellent for softer soils, it does offer a number of disadvantages. First, it can be a source of heat loss in colder climates. With the container seated right against the concrete, heat escapes easily. Therefore, you will need a thick layer of insulation on the lower surface and floor of the container. Second, as mentioned before, you'll have to dig quite a bit to prepare the soil for a slab-on-grade. Finally, you'll have to place the utilities before you pour, and you will not have external access to the lines once the concrete has hardened.

Despite these disadvantages, the slab-on-grade foundation offers a great degree of stability, and the lack of space between container and foundation makes it less susceptible to pests like termites.

Typically, with a raft foundation, you will want to give a depth of 2 ft. below your desired elevation and extend 2 ft. beyond the edges of your structure. These requirements will vary with soil type and with the special conditions of your site. Offered below is a diagram that provides a visual of the raft foundation both before and after a structure has been placed upon it.

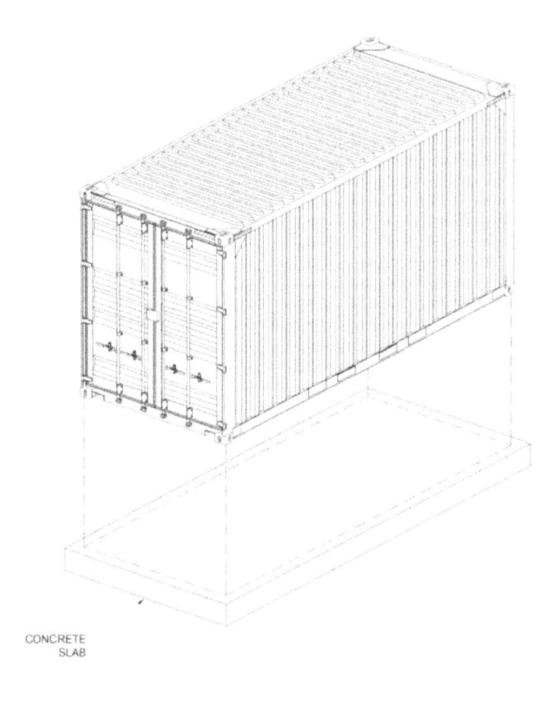

Important: If using a slab-on-grade foundation, make sure that your utilities are placed before pouring or you won't be able to access the area necessary to place your lines.

Trench Foundation

The trench foundation is also known as the spread footing or strip foundation. Essentially, it combines the qualities of the pier and raft foundation, providing a solid foundation beneath the entire edge of the structure. With all of the container's exterior walls supported, the weight is distributed over a larger area than with the pier or piling foundations.

Areas of poor drainage can be benefited by using a variant of this foundation known as the "rubble trench." If you place a layer of gravel or loose stone beneath the concrete base, then water is allowed to escape while the load of the structure is held secure.

The diagram below demonstrates the appropriate placement of the trench foundation:

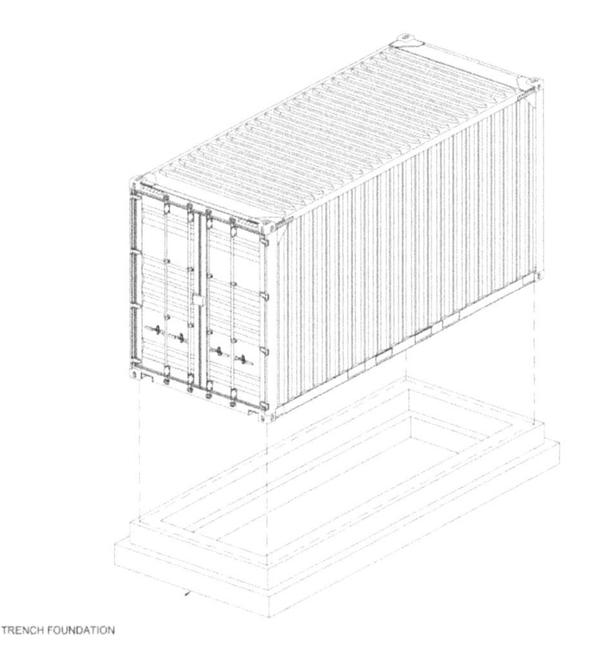

A few notes: The trench, pier, and raft foundations require a minimum of 50cm of depth. You will also want to ensure that both trench and raft foundations extend at least a foot beyond the edge of the structure. For the trench foundation, ensure that the inner edge of the footing also extends at least a foot inwardly past the inner edge of the structure.

Preparing and Placing Your Concrete

Concrete is a beautiful building material to work with, offering the potential to be formed into any shape desired and high compressive strength. However, you must know a few details to make sure that you can place it effectively and ensure it cures to the desired strength.

First, a few things about what concrete actually is: concrete is a combination between cement, gravel, and sand. When cement mixes with water, a chemical reaction ensues. The cement hardens as the water evaporates, trapping the sand and gravel within the matrix of the hardened cement. This combination offers a high degree of compressive strength. In other words, it can take quite a bit of pressure without a loss of integrity. The process of water evaporation and chemical hardening is called "curing" and is the process whereby concrete attains its full compressive strength.

The strength of your concrete depends upon the ratio of cement to aggregate. The final strength of a concrete mix is indicated in ready-mixes by a C-value. All-purpose concrete has a strength of C-15 and utilizes a mix of one-part cement to two parts sand and five parts gravel. To create concrete with a strength of C-30, simply combine one-part cement to two parts sand and three parts gravel. The report of the geotechnical engineer will determine the necessary strength of concrete for your foundation.

Small quantities of concrete can be mixed by hand or with a cement mixer. For anything larger than one cubic meter, it may be more efficient to have the concrete delivered to the site. If mixing the elements by hand, ensure that they are thoroughly combined. Otherwise, the strength of the resulting concrete will suffer.

Calculating the necessary volume of concrete is a simple matter of determining the volume of your desired placement. The one thing to remember is that concrete volume is calculated in cubic meters. Here are a few sample calculations for a single 40-ft. container to help you get the idea:

Pier Foundations: 6 x (50cm)3 = 6 x 125,000cm3 = 750,000cm3

1,000,000cm3 = 1m3 → 750,000cm3 = .75m3

Raft Foundation: (40+2) ft x (8+2) ft x 2ft = 840ft3

1ft3 = .283m3 → 840ft3 = 23.72m3

Trench Foundation: (40+2) ft x 2ft x 2ft + (8-2) ft x 2ft x2ft → 168ft3 + 24ft3 → 192ft3

1ft3 = .283m3 → 192ft3 = 5.44m3

It may take some math to get there, but with a small amount of planning, you'll know exactly how much concrete you'll need.

Give your concrete five to seven days after placement to cure to full strength.

If you're placing concrete in warm weather, moisten the soil with cold water before you pour, mix the cement with cold water, and shade the concrete after placement. You can also place the concrete in the late evening or early morning to avoid high heat during the most sensitive curing times.

If pouring in extreme cold, make sure to clear any snow, ice, or standing water before placing the concrete. Cover the concrete with insulating blankets once it has been placed. Once the concrete has cured, remove the blankets gradually to prevent cracking from rapid temperature changes.

Tip: Another option is to place a steel plate upon the corners of the foundation before the concrete sets. This will increase the strength of your foundation and allow you to weld the container securely to it.

Site Preparation Checklist

- Get a geoengineering soil profile.
- Determine the most appropriate foundation type and depth.
- Meet with a structural engineer to design the foundation.
- Decide if you can pour the foundation yourself or if you need a contractor. If you do need a contractor for the job, hire well.
- Calculate the concrete strength required for the job.
- Make calculations to determine the volume of concrete to pour the foundation
- Dig the foundation.
- Place the molds.
- Place a gridwork of rebar and steel wire into the molds to reinforce and offer flexural stability to the concrete once it has cured.
- Mix concrete to the necessary strength and pour it into the molds, ensuring that the foundation is level.
- Pour with your weather conditions in mind, ensuring that the concrete is able to maintain a stable temperature as it cures.
- Allow the concrete to cure from five to seven days before placement.

4.3 Converting Your Container – On or Offsite?

Converting your container means making the necessary modifications to create the shell of your living space. One important consideration here is whether you'll be making the necessary modifications to convert your container to a dwelling on-site or if the conversion will be done elsewhere.

Certain designs require walls to be removed so that containers can be connected to create larger spaces. Doorways, arches, and windows must also be cut through the steel. Some of these modifications will require equipment, such as welding tools, cutting torches, grinders, heavy-duty drills, and sprayers for insulation. Occasionally, it is more economical to have the containers delivered to a workshop supplied with the necessary tools.

On the other hand, having the containers delivered directly to the site and making the modifications in place can save you an additional shipping cost. The catch is that you need access to the necessary tools and skills to make this option work for you. Both onsite and offsite conversion offer pros and cons. Following is an in-depth look at both alternatives, and a mention of a third option that you may find useful.

Onsite Conversion

If you can manage the conversion onsite, it is helpful for several reasons.

The first is that you will have uninterrupted access to the site. You can make your own hours when converting your shipping container to a home. And, perhaps worthy of mentioning first, once you have converted your container, it is already in place and won't require any further travel.

Modifying containers too deeply could compromise their structural integrity to some degree. This isn't an issue if they are already in place; however, if they are converted offsite, then you will have to be doubly careful in transit. Onsite conversion avoids this issue altogether.

There are a few challenges associated with onsite conversion. First, you'll need to have the tools and skills to do the conversion in place. If you intend to purchase the tools specifically for this job, this can be an expensive option. Plus, if you're building on a greenfield site, you'll need to supply power and water.

This often means a generator, which can be noisy and expensive. You can also choose to have electric facilities established before placement, though this will have to be planned out ahead of time.

If you choose to convert your containers in place, the available option is to contract a construction team for the conversion process. This sidesteps the need to buy costly tools and makes sure that you have the necessary skills at hand to make the conversion. However, it is more expensive than a DIY project. This is an ideal option if you lack the necessary tools and skills and if it is unfeasible to station your containers at a local workshop to convert them.

Offsite Conversion

If you aren't well supplied with tools, then one good option is to have the containers delivered to a local workshop or fabricator. Once they are delivered, you can use the tools supplied there to make all necessary modifications before transporting them to your building site.

In addition to the tools, you'll have many experienced people on hand that can help you with any details that require a bit more know-how.

One big advantage is that workshops provide protection from the rain and the elements.

You will not have to be concerned about immediately making sure your containers are watertight. They will also be protected overnight, so you won't have to worry about tampering or interference when you are unable to be onsite. Finally, while at a workshop, you will have access to water and power, which means you won't have to set up supplies before delivery.

Although offsite modification offers a number of advantages, there are also a few disadvantages to consider. First, the location of the workshop might be fairly distant from you, requiring a hefty commute to and from it to work on the modifications. Second, the workshop is unlikely to be open at all hours. This means that you may find yourself limited in your access to the container, especially if you are working a regular job in the process. Look into the times that the workshop or fabricator will be open before deciding to use it for your modifications, and try to arrange a flat fee for the month or the week if possible.

A third option is to have your containers converted before delivery. This will be more expensive than either of the previous options; however, you will be able to save quite a bit of time and place your containers directly once they are delivered. Purchasing your containers pre-converted will also ensure that they are both modified and delivered professionally and that they make their way into place intact and without damage.

4.4 Container Delivery

Once you have decided how to modify your container and made all necessary site preparations, it's time to nail down the details for container delivery. You already know where your container is going.

How is it going to get there?

Local dealers offer several advantages in this respect. First and foremost, most local dealers operate in conjunction with a freight service that can handle the delivery. Furthermore, they can help to ensure that all the containers you purchase come from the same company.

This helps to avoid differences intolerance concerning internal and external dimensions. Despite this, you can sometimes cut costs by contracting an external freight service. To get the best deal, you'll have to shop around and explore your options.

New Containers

If you are purchasing your new containers, they will cost a bit more, but they are sure to come in good condition. However, you will want to seek out a supplier relatively close to you. Otherwise, you may end up paying as much for the shipping as you do for the containers themselves. Shipping your containers new requires you to pay the full delivery cost. However, opting for the one-time use ensures that you get good-as-new containers and that the bulk of the shipping cost is paid by the company receiving their cargo.

In order to give you an idea of the importance of this decision, shipping new containers from a remote location like China may cost from $2,000 – $23,000, just to have them arrive at a nearby port. At the other hand, if you choose a one-time-use container, you can have them arrive at no cost to yourself. The only thing to consider into your budget is the cost of getting the containers from the port to the building site.

Shipping Costs

As indicated above, shipping costs will vary greatly depending upon the origin of the container. Some estimates include $230 to transport a 20-ft. container for 50 miles and offloading it, $420 for a similar delivery of a 40-ft. container, and $400 for 300-mile transportation of 20-ft. containers. Clearly, this will depend upon the shipping company, the number of containers, and the conditions surrounding their journey.

One thing to remember is to make sure that you have arranged the containers with plenty of time for delivery. Shipping companies sometimes need from weeks to months to make a delivery, depending upon their distance. Also, the most frequently deal in bulk, so the few shipping containers you need to build your home won't be their highest priority. Try to make the arrangements early so that the containers will arrive when your site is prepared and ready for modification.

Another tip that can save you quite a bit of money is to remember to shop around.

The shipping costs can differ quite a bit from one company to another, so if you explore several options, you can make sure to get the best price given your circumstances.

4.5 Placing Your Container

Tilting the Container into Place

Once your container reaches the site, there are a few options for placing it.

The cheapest option is for the container to be delivered on a flatbed trailer. If the site allows, you may be able to have the driver tilt the bed and slide the container directly onto the foundation. This is also the easiest way to go, and if you can plan your design and site layout to make it a possibility, then you will be able to save the price of renting either a crane or HIAB. To do so, you will have to arrange the foundation so that there is the space of a flatbed trailer and truck adjacent to the narrow end of the foundation, leaving space for the truck to maneuver.

Placing with Crane or HIAB

Sometimes, tilting the container onto the foundation is simply not an option.

Also, the tilting option is unfeasible if your construction is more complicated or multi-level. If so, then you will need to lift your container(s) and set it upon the foundation. A HIAB is cheaper, and it will work for smaller containers. However, it may be unable to lift anything more than a 20-ft. container. A crane, though more expensive, will have sufficient lifting power and control for heavier containers and more delicate operations. The typical price for crane rental is $700 per day, though this will depend upon the contractor.

Lining and Insulation

One important tip when placing your containers upon the foundation is to line them with a polyethylene damp-proof membrane. Also, if you use a crane or HIAB, you will have access to the underside of the containers. You can lift them one by one, sandblast the bottom, and add a 1 in. coating of polyurethane spray-foam insulation. This will reduce heat loss from the bottom of the container. Even without the benefit of a crane or HIAB, you can treat the underside of the container if using a concrete pier foundation.

Tip: If your foundation isn't completely level, you may need to use shims, metal spacers to raise the container and bring it level.

Tip: By spraying foam insulation between any connecting walls once the containers have been lined up, you can keep moisture out, reduce drafts, and help maintain the internal temperature of the containers.

Cleaning the Containers

Once you have placed your containers, you'll begin to see the shell of your home shaping up. The next step is to connect them. First, however, they will need to be thoroughly cleaned. This will be more important for used containers than new or one-time use. The sandblaster and pressure washer are the quickest options for cleaning; however, in a pinch, you can use a grinder or even wire wool. Make sure to clean the inside of the container, including the wooden flooring. Then proceed to the outer walls and roof of the container.

Stabilizing the Containers on the Foundation

In most cases, the weight of the container alone will be sufficient to seat the container firmly upon the foundation. However, if you have chosen to place steel plates into the surface of the concrete on the corners of the foundation, the containers can be welded to the plates to stabilize them further.

Another option is to bolt the containers to the foundation. To do this, you will want to drill through the bottom corner fittings of the container into the piers, piles, trench, or slab.

Once the hole has been drilled, a 12 in. by 1 in. bolt can be placed through the hole. Make sure that you use a washer around the head

of the bolt to seat it firmly to the bottom of the container. Then hammer the bolt into the hole you have drilled. To achieve the final snug, tighten the head of the bolt.

You will only need one bolt in the corner of each container to ensure that they are solid and secure

4.6 Connecting the Containers

Once the containers have been placed and bolted or welded to the foundation, it's time to connect them securely to one another. You have three options at this point: bolt, weld, or clamp.

Clamping

The least secure (and least expensive) of the three is to clamp the containers together.

It does offer the option of disconnecting the containers from one another in the future, should that be desired.

However, given that they have already been bolted securely in place, other options should be used if at all possible.

Bolting

Bolting the containers together is the next option. It is more secure than clamping and only slightly more expensive.

If you opt for this option, the containers should be bolted together at the adjacent corners. Drill through the corner fitting points from one container to the next. You will also want to drill through a metal plate. This will act as a washer for the threaded side of the bolt. Insert the bolt through the hole (including a washer), slide it through the containers, and then place the metal plate, an additional washer, and a nut on the threaded end. Torque the nut tight, and then seal any gaps by placing mastic around both ends of the bolt.

Welding

Like clamping, bolting leaves, the option of disassembling the containers later should the need require. However, the best option by far is welding. Welding makes the overall structure more rigid and secure. It also helps to keep the containers level despite settling. If you have access to the equipment and tools, then welding is by far the best option for a long-lasting shipping container home with a minimum of repairs needed over its lifetime.

The containers should be welded at the jointure of the roof, floor, and end walls.

One of the best methods is to place a 3-in. x 1/8-in. Length of flat steel against the jointure of the roofs and secure it with a stitch weld. Once this has been welded in place, repeat the process for each end wall with a 2-in. x 1/8-in. Length of flat steel. Finally, use another 2-in. x 1/8-in. Piece of flat steel to weld together any overlapping floors of adjoining containers. This will ensure that all of the contact points between containers are welded securely to one another.

Tip: To prevent rust, place a few layers of latex paint over each of the flat steel bars.

Make sure to completely cover the area of the weld.

Conversion Plan, Delivery, Placement, and Connection Checklist

- Shop around to get many quotes for container shipping.
- Decide whether to convert the containers onsite or offsite and plan your delivery accordingly.
- Arrange container delivery.
- Explore the site and design to determine whether crane, flatbed, or HIAB are most appropriate for placement.
- If possible, insulate the bottoms of the containers prior to placement.
- After placing the containers, secure them to the foundation with bolts or welds.
- Spray foam insulation between adjoining walls.
- Connect the containers securely to one another with clamps, bolts, or welds.

4.7 Insulation

Insulation is undoubtedly one of the most important aspects to consider when building a container home, and the construction steps in which you will need to consider this aspect are several.

In this chapter, however, we will discuss insulation in a generic way, in order to give you a general knowledge of the topic before going into the details of the individual construction steps.

You'll find specific details on what to do, and what techniques are best to use, in each section that will discuss the construction steps that may involve working on insulating your container home.

Would you air-condition an open-air porch or patio that becomes too hot in the summer? Of course, not without first surrounding it with walls. Separate the conditioned air (air that has been deliberately chilled or warmed, depending on the season) from the outside air. Otherwise, you're air cooling the neighborhood (as your parents may have noticed when you left the front door open!)

The walls surrounding your porch made of newspaper or plastic food wrap would be ineffective at controlling the temperature. A thin wall will not be able to effectively block heat transmission from the heated to the cool side. While real air cannot get through the wall, the heat contained in the air may. So, despite the separation of the air, your energy efficiency would be very poor.

As a result, insulation is a substance created to keep heat from passing through the walls (and floor and ceiling) of your container home. Air or other gases are trapped in a complex matrix of small cells or passageways.

Gases conduct heat energy poorly compared to solids and liquids, making them good insulators. The function of convection inside the gas is reduced by restricting the gases to millions of small cells, further enhancing the material's insulating characteristics.

When we speak of thermal insulation, we almost always refer to conductive (and to a lesser degree, convective) heat flow. An "R-value" is used to assess the resistance to heat flow, which is also how insulation is evaluated (higher is better).

Why does your container need insulation?

For pleasant, energy-efficient living, every house must be insulated, but a steel shipping container home offers several particular challenges:

Condensation: inside an unsecured metal shipping container, condensation may make it seem like you're in a tropical jungle. Condensation will form when heated air comes into touch with the cool metal. Water vapor may pass through conventionally framed walls like water passing through a submarine's screen door. Mold, rust, and corrosion are all caused by moisture.

Radiant Heat and Cold: metal is a great heat and cold conductor. The metal will get chilly in the winter, making the inside of your container house seem like an icebox. In warmer weather, the sun's rays will rapidly radiate heat through the steel sheets, making the container uncomfortably hot and damp.

Where to place your container insulation?

The walls of most building types contain several layers of materials. The material you see on the inside is not the same as what you see on the exterior. Several layers of materials provide structure, weatherproofing, fire resistance, thermal insulation, vapor barrier, and other functions in between.

The container actually is one of these layers in shipping container houses. In addition, you must decide where the container skin will be placed inside the overall wall system.

The most common solution is to install insulation inside the shipping container's inner walls. Most designs have stud walls as a location to conduct plumbing and electrical lines, as well as a point of attachment for drywall or other interior surfaces. It's just common sense to insulate the spaces between the studs. Then, if you wish, you may very much leave the container's outside alone.

However, external insulation may be a better match for certain individuals. In this instance, you'll need to put insulation outside the container and then cover it with weather-resistant sheathing. For individuals who wish to cover or hide the shipping containers themselves, this offers greater internal room and a more controlled external look.

Types of shipping container insulation

We'll go over five different types of insulation in this section, all of which are classified by the physical shape they take, which is directly linked to how they're applied. Similar to how peanut butter and peanuts (or applesauce and apples, or we'll just stop there!) may fall into two distinct food groups. Some insulating materials, such as polyurethane foam and cellulose, may fall into more than one of the categories below if they may be bought and installed in various ways.

Recognizing the distinctions between materials and understanding how they impact your particular circumstances is the essential aspect of selecting the right kind of insulation for your needs. With that stated, let's have a look at the various choices.

Non-traditional insulation

This type of insulation is composed of unusual materials that are typically selected at least in part for their environmental friendliness and are often referred to as "cheap" insulation. Because of their low R-value per inch, they are less appropriate for most owners unless environmental friendliness is your first priority and you are prepared to sacrifice interior space for it.

While they are definitely cost-effective insulating options, their usefulness is usually limited. They may be appropriate for more mild climates with less severe temperature changes.

Straw Bale: A straw bale piled like blocks, similar to the kind you'd use to feed a horse. Because of the size of straw bales, this would only work for container insulation on the outside.

Hempcrete: is a substance composed of hemp that is comparable to concrete but has less strength.

Blanket insulation

Blanket insulation comes in the shape of batts (pre-cut lengths to suit common wall heights) and rolls (large rolled-up sections that must be cut to length during installation). It's "fluffy," compressible, and not self-supporting. It's similar to a blanket you'd use to stay warm in your home on a cold winter evening, but it's thicker and composed of different materials. Blanket insulation is usually often made up of long fibers mashed together in a compact area, essentially making it open-celled.

Blanket insulation is designed to be attached in the spaces between studs, and it relies on the studs for structural stiffness since it would otherwise collapse into a pile if not supported. It is among the cheapest choices and is simple to install, needing just a stapler to attach to studs.

Blanket insulation comes in a variety of forms, including:

Fiberglass insulation: is made of tiny fibers produced from superheated sand or recycled glass. This is the most popular kind of low-cost wall insulation in Western nations.

Insulation produced from minerals/ceramics or slag, a byproduct of metal manufacturing, is known as slag wool, mineral wool, or rock wool.

Sheep Wool Insulation: sheep wool insulation is exactly what it sounds like insulation produced from the shorn wool of sheep.

Cotton or Denim Insulation: made mostly of recycled denim or blue jeans, cotton insulation is typically blueish in hue. More expensive, but with a large proportion of recycled materials.

Blanket insulation is permeable to water vapor, which may be reduced using a vapor retarder in conventional construction. Vapor retarders, on the other hand, are generally not a smart option for container houses since the outside metal shell is already a vapor barrier, and by adding a second barrier, you risk trapping water vapor in the wall cavities.

Some blanket insulation fibers, most notably fiberglass, may irritate the eyes, skin, and respiratory systems. Before handling these materials, use proper PPE (personal protective equipment) such as a dust mask, gloves, and safety glasses. For appropriate handling methods, see the MSDS (Material Safety Data Sheet) or any instructions on the product package.

Expanded Foam Insulation

Expanded foam is pre-sized for common wall heights and produced off-site into big boards and insulation panels. These insulation panels, unlike blanket insulation, are self-supporting. Cutting is used to creating holes for items like doors and windows on-site. Similar to spray foam insulation, gas may escape the cells in closed cell expanded foam variations, resulting in a lower R-value over time.

Expanded foam is easy to work with and maybe bonded directly to the container or connected to studs. Assuming you have not many cuts to make, it may be quite fast to install. Some are molded to look like the corrugations on the side of a cargo container. You'll have huge air gaps in these corrugated regions if you don't

.

Different types of foam insulation

Open-cell polyurethane foam insulation (oc PU Foam): has a spongy feel and a lower than average R-value because the foam cells are not as thick and are filled with air.

The 'blowing agent' fills the small microscopic cells with a gas other than air that has superior heat conduction characteristics, raising the R-value of the foam.

Extruded Polystyrene Foam Insulation (EPS): is a closed-cell foam made up of tiny plastic beads fused together. It's the white foam you've probably seen in items like coffee cups, and it's what businesses like InSoFast use in their shipping container insulation kits.

Expanded Polystyrene Foam Insulation (XPS): is made from molten polystyrene that is pressed into closed-cell foam sheets. While the term is close to EPS, it is not the same.

Polyisocyanurate (Polyiso): is a stiff polyurethane that is similar to polyurethane.

Spray insulation

Spray insulation comes in a variety of materials, all of which are applied by spraying or pumping a liquid combination that hardens into a solid. Spray insulation is continuous and extends into nooks, crevices, and gaps because of how it is sprayed and clings to itself. This creates a barrier that prevents both air movement and heat transmission.

Spray foam insulation expands when it is applied and subsequently solidifies, aiding in the sealing process. However, since the foam will expand beyond the face of your studs, it will need to be trimmed.

Different types of spray foam insulation

Open-Cell Spray Polyurethane Foam: (ocSPF) is a less desirable kind of polyurethane spray foam insulation because it allows air to flow between cells, resulting in a lower R-value per inch.

Closed-Cell Spray Polyurethane Foam: (ccSPF): This is the most popular shipping container insulation. This spray foam insulation has one of the highest R-values per inch and works well as a vapor barrier. Off-gassing after spray application is a problem, so check with your manufacturer for cure periods and also how long it will take before you can move in. The gas in these closed-cell versions may sometimes escape the cells, resulting in a lower R-value over time.

Non-expanding sprayed-in insulation: is a different but similar approach. Unlike the other spray foam insulation kinds, it does not chemically expand when applied, but it does move about to fully fill the space.

Damp-Spray Cellulose Insulation: is made from shredded recycled paper materials. Rather than using a standard blown-in application, a specific rig that adds water or adhesives at the time of application (known as damp-spraying), may be used to bind the cellulose together and allow it to be applied to open-sided wall cavities.

Cementitious Foam Insulation: is a very light combination of water, air, and natural minerals that mimics concrete when cured but looks like shaving cream when applied and may be brittle after curing if not handled carefully. Despite having a lower R-value than spray foam insulation, cementitious foam is eco-friendly, non-toxic, and non-flammable due to its components.

As you can see, there are a lot of choices to choose from. Choosing the right insulation for you requires a thorough knowledge of your individual decision-making variables, such as budget, climate, design, and personal heat and cold tolerance.

If by any chance you are unsure how to do it, look at what others in your region are currently doing. Using materials that are already prevalent in your area is frequently simpler and less expensive. A discussion with a local contractor to obtain site-specific suggestions and guidance may also be beneficial.

4.8 Building Walls and Ceilings

The materials for building walls are pretty simple. First, you'll need 2" by 3" studs. The 1" smaller width, compared to a 2" by 4" stud, is simply to give you more space in your limited space. Next, you'll need your drywall. To save space, you'll also want to go thin on your drywall. A 7/16" thickness is about as thin as you can go without being extremely fragile. Lastly, you'll need drywall screws, plenty of drywall mud, and the right tape and trowels to apply the mud.

Before you begin constructing walls, you'll need to decide how you want to insulate your outside walls. Depending on your preference, you can insulate the outside or the inside walls. Spray foaming the inside of the wall is typically easier, as it only requires foam, some studs, and drywall. If you insulate the outside, you have to frame, insulate, and cover the walls with some sort of weatherproof outer sheeting. For a shipping container home, insulating the inside of the wall is ideal.

Assuming we stick to our example and are insulating the inside walls of our 20' shipping container, we first have to attach some sort of studs or 1" strips to give us something to screw the drywall to. An easy method is to lay 2" by 4" boards in the recessed grooves of the shipping container wall. Toenail your screws or shoot them at an angle into the floor. For the tops, you may consider tying in the same style boards to give yourself something to shoot your ceiling boards too. In this case, you are basically making an arch up the wall, across the ceiling, and back down the wall on the other side.

You will space your studs every 2'. This will give adequate support to both the walls and ceiling and will let you break your 4' wide sheets perfectly as you lay them down the container. Keep in mind; you'll have to either frame around your ductwork or have the ductwork run exposed in front of the wall.

To choose the best way to do it, you have to consider the kind of ductwork you have added and the aesthetic result you want to achieve. If you are satisfied with the extra space, it takes up, an easy way to build walls that is more similar to traditional construction is to add either a 2" thick or 1" thick board that runs the entire length of the top and bottom of the wall. These are called top and bottom plates. You simply lay them out, nail or screw studs every 2', and then put the other end in the same way. You lean the wall up and secure to the floor and run the ceiling studs or rafters across the top. This method is simple, effective, and ensures everything is secure. Even so, with the ribbed shape of a shipping container wall, this will stick out farther and take up more of your limited space. If you have an 8' wide shipping container, the outside interior walls could reduce your inner width dimension by up to 8".

Once your outer wall framing is secure, you can begin to prepare your electrical boxes for outlets and switches. Be sure that all electrical outlets and switch boxes are in their desired position and properly mounted to the stud. Double-check their measurements to ensure all of your outlets are a uniform height and the same for your switches. The boxes used for electrical outlets and switches should sit flush with the front of the stud. This way, as you set your drywall sheets on the wall, you can simply mark their location to be routed out later. If you do not have a router and do not want to spend the money, a handheld drywall saw is a good alternative.

Before you begin hanging drywall, sweep or vacuum thoroughly to remove dust and debris. Drywall sheets sitting on a piece of debris can crack or not sit flat on the studs. If you plan to one day move your container again, you may consider adding some strong construction adhesive or wood glue to the studs before you place your drywall sheets. Adhesive, in combination with drywall screws, give the walls extra strength, especially if the container is moving around. Either way, your 4' by 8' drywall sheets can either be placed horizontally or vertically. With 2' spaced studs, your sheets will meet at a stud regardless. You never want a piece of drywall to end without a stud behind it.

As you secure your drywall, you will place your screws every 6-8" on the outer perimeter of your sheets and about every 12" in the studs on the inside. If you are using adhesive, be sure to apply it just before setting the sheet, as it will dry quickly. As you come to corners or unique features in your home, you may have to cut your drywall sheets. Utilize a framing square or long straight edge of some sort to mark your cut and score it with a utility knife. Once scored, drywall will break fairly easily where you can run your knife through again to separate it.

When you have the drywall installed on your walls, you can begin installing drywall on your ceiling. However, before you begin putting drywall sheets up in the ceiling, you need to make sure that you have either properly insulated your ceiling or made a firm decision to insulate the outside and cover it with a roof. You also need to make sure all your wiring or even plumbing that may be up in the ceiling is run. More specifically, anywhere you want, a light fixture must have the proper wiring in the right location.

In your ceiling, light fixtures will require a cup-shaped box used for mounting lights or even ceiling fans. The cup will mount to the rafter, and the wiring simply needs to poke through and hang out until after the drywall is installed. If you have any air ducts running in the ceiling, you'll want to mark their location so they can be cut out later.

Ceiling drywall sheets can be installed very similarly to the sheets on the outer walls. This may require some help to hold the boards up while another person secures them with screws. You'll definitely need at least a small ladder for this work. Glue or adhesive is beneficial for the ceiling in the same way it was for the outer walls. Once the ceiling boards are installed, a hole saw can be used to cut through the drywall where any light fixtures or vents were to be installed.

Interior walls are installed in much the same way as outer walls. You will want to decide what doors you can acquire and what size you prefer to use. This is important to know for framing any interior wall with a door. You will maintain a 2' space between studs except where needed to mount things like shelves, tie-in cabinets, and door frames. Setting walls can be tricky when considering all the different things that may go on in your home.

Maintain peace of mind that all things can be repaired or renovated. Take it slow and think things through before you start working.

This book can give you a basic outline, but only you possess your vision and what unique opportunities are staring you in the face. Often, people will opt to not use adhesive or glue for interior walls until they are at least half drywalled. This way, if you don't like something, you can undo it without chipping away at any glue.

The final step of building an interior wall is to apply tape and mud to the joints. You will be faced with 3 different types of joints when building walls. There are inside joints, outside joints, and butt joints. If you look at the corner of a room, that is an inside joint. An outside joint is where a wall turns into an open space, such as leading into a doorway or down a hallway. Butt joints are all the joints where your drywall sheets come together. Butt joints do not have an angle to them.

To begin taping and mudding, you must first purchase the right type of mud from a hardware store. Mud can be purchased pre-mixed or as a powder that can be mixed to your desired thickness. If you have no experience with mud, it is probably easiest to buy the pre-mixed type. In addition to the mud, you need to purchase drywall tape, pre-made outside corners, trowels to spread the mud, and a sanding block and sandpaper.

Taping and mudding are fairly simple but can take a while to get used to. For any joint, spread a liberal amount of mud into the joint and spread evenly. Next, run a piece of tape from the floor to the ceiling, or use a premade corner for outside corner joints. Lightly press the tape into the mud and ensure the moisture from the mud soaks into the tape. Ensuring the tape is straight, moist, and flat, apply an additional layer of mud. Spread this final layer of mud widely to help blend the joint in with the wall. Be sure to have enough mud for your purpose. It' s better to have too much than too little. It can be tricky getting the mud to be as smooth as you want, but you'll get the hang of it with practice.

After giving the mud about a day to dry, the next day, you can sand the mud down to help achieve your desired smoothness and perfection. If needed, mud can be added and reapplied. If you are satisfied with your mud, your wall should be ready for primer and paint.

The process is very much the same to mud your ceiling. The main difference is, instead of preparing for paint, many people will opt for a textured ceiling. To do this, simply find mud specifically for ceilings and purchase a ceiling stomping brush. The light ceiling mud can be applied with a paint roller and then stomped with the brush to give a rough textured look. This process can be very messy, so plan accordingly to have plastic or drop cloth to protect the floor and any items you've brought in your house.

4.9 Planning the installation of cabinets, electrical outlets and appliances

In our last section we talked about how to build walls and ceilings in your home. We discovered that the you need to be mindful of wiring and where things are going to go; things like light switches and plugs. This leads to other choices like your cabinets. Many more modern designs have integrated lights, and that means a power source is needed somewhere. The correct planning will make all of the next steps a breeze. Even if you think you've got it covered, there might be areas that have been missed and you don't want that to happen. Sure, drywall is easy enough to repair, but it's much easier to prevent the problems, so let's discuss how you can go about that.

Start with the lights. These are going to be a critical component in the layout. So, putting in light boxes first will make the whole process run a lot more smoothly. This gives you a more defined idea on the layout, and it allows you the opportunity to test out these switches before they get sealed in and become hard to access.

But electrical problems aren't the only ones you should think about in advance to prevent them from happening. There is also the water supply, particularly when it comes to bathrooms and kitchens, so be sure to decide early on where the pipes will go. These in and out lines will need to go in before the floor does, and with hardy and easily cracked floor coverings like tiles, you don't want to have to move them more than is totally necessary.

Once the fixtures are in, it's time to get the floor down, then it's onto the fun part of designing; the sink, bath, cabinets, fridge – all of those choices that make a house a home.

When you're putting the cabinets in, you're going to want to make sure they're lined up straight and tightly secured. This means using a plum line, spirit level and screws which are 2 to 3 inches long. You'll need to get through any fresh aster and hit solid wall to make them secure. Should you find that you have made a mistake, try to fix it with a shim, and anything else is easy to hide with a vase. Of course, it's better to hide any scuffs out of sight and to keep the surfaces nice and pristine. You won't regret making a little tidy up.

It's only after the cabinet is properly secured to the wall that it is time to connect the plumbing. This way you have the most opportunity to get things lined up before making the final touches. You'll also need to connect the sewage or septic line at this point. This is where it can get a little tricky, but it is doable. What you'll need to do next is to fit your 'P-trap' under the sink. This is done in order to avoid sewer gasses seeping up into your house, and let's be real here, nobody wants that. Since P-traps are the curvy bend under your loo where water sits, there's an extra pressure to get it right. This water is the blockade between you and those unpleasant smells, so make sure that it's screwed in tight.

The toilet is the final touch then and luckily, these come in nearly one piece which makes them quick and easy to pop into place and anchor down.

After that, you can just sit and enjoy your new space. Its as easy as that, and remember, planning is what makes it perfect.

4.10 Building the Roof

Building a roof onto your shipping container home is a matter of preference.

The easiest solution is to use the flat roof, the roof of the container itself. While this will save quite a bit on both construction costs and time, it does leave your container susceptible to pooling and rust.

The flat roof also offers very little insulation. Since heat rises, most of the heat will be lost from the top. To top it off, the container itself is made out of steel. It will collect both heat and cold and transfer it to the interior. Without insulation, you could be paying an arm and a leg in heating and cooling during more extreme weather.

Other options for roofing will help to add additional insulation, provide a layer of protection from pooling water, and offer overhangs to keep water from dripping down the windows. Some alternatives for roofing styles are the shed roof and the gable roof. The construction methods for each style are explored below, along with a discussion of the benefits of each.

Roofing Styles

Flat Roof

As mentioned above, the flat roof is the easiest, quickest, and cheapest option.

It requires little to no modification, as you are simply using the metal roof of the container. This option will be more than sufficient for most purposes. However, there are certain measures that should be taken to ensure the longevity and comfort of your dwelling.

The drawbacks of a flat roof have been addressed above. The first is the pooling of water on the roof from the rain. This can lead to rust and to the loss of structural integrity. One easy solution is to place a tarpaulin over the roof of the container. This can then be covered with rolls of asphalt.

This will weigh the tarpaulin in place and offer an additional layer of defense against the elements.

The asphalt will then need to be fixed into place. When covering the roof of the container, make sure to leave an overhang of at least 2 in. You can then bolt 2-in. x 1/8 in. Steel bar into the top of the container through the asphalt. Make sure to seal the bolt holes with mastic so that you don't have leakage during heavy rains.

Before installing your tarpaulin and asphalt protective layer, you may choose to cover the roof with a 1-in. thick layer of spray foam. This will offer a certain degree of insulation; however, you will want to add to this by installing a ceiling and insulating this as well.

Offered below is a simple diagram that demonstrates the flat roof option for your shipping container home:

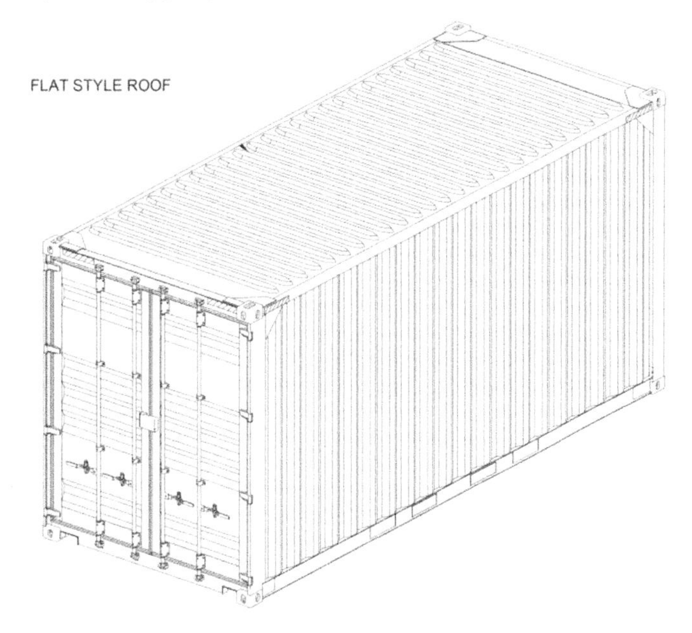

Shed Roof

The roof of your shed is simply a single slope, slanted downward from one end to the other. This is a low-cost and simple-to-build structure that takes days or less to complete from start to finish. Another advantage of this choice is that it is well-suited to the installation of solar panels. If you prefer to add a constructed roof to your home, this involves a little more in the way of tools, resources, and know-how, but it is the cheapest and easiest alternative.

Offered below is a simple diagram that shows the basic design of the shed roof:

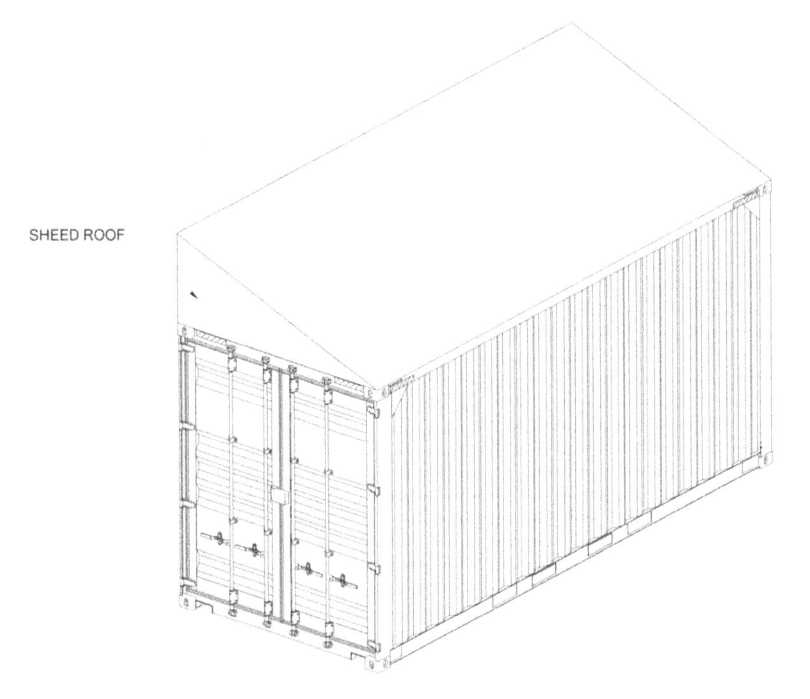

Installation

Welding correct-angle steel bars to the width of the container from both sides is the first stage in constructing a shed roof. After that, you'll need to attach a wooden joint to the plate's elevated flange: 2x6 beams are appropriate for this application and will be utilized to secure the trusses.

The trusses should be spaced approximately 18 inches apart.

This implies that a 20-foot container will need 14 trusses, whereas a 40-foot container would require 28.

Make careful you utilize a skew nailing method while fastening the trusses. At each location, hammer two nails into the truss at an angle of 25 degrees from the vertical. This produces an x-shape that keeps the trusses in place even when lateral pressure is applied.

The general form of the roof will be evident after the trusses have been fastened.

The next stage is to line the trusses' angles with 20-foot-long purlins, which are beams that form a level surface across the trusses' angles.

Purlins should be spaced about 1 foot apart. After that, brace the truss to protect them from the wind's pressure. The figure below depicts the first step of constructing a shed-style roof:

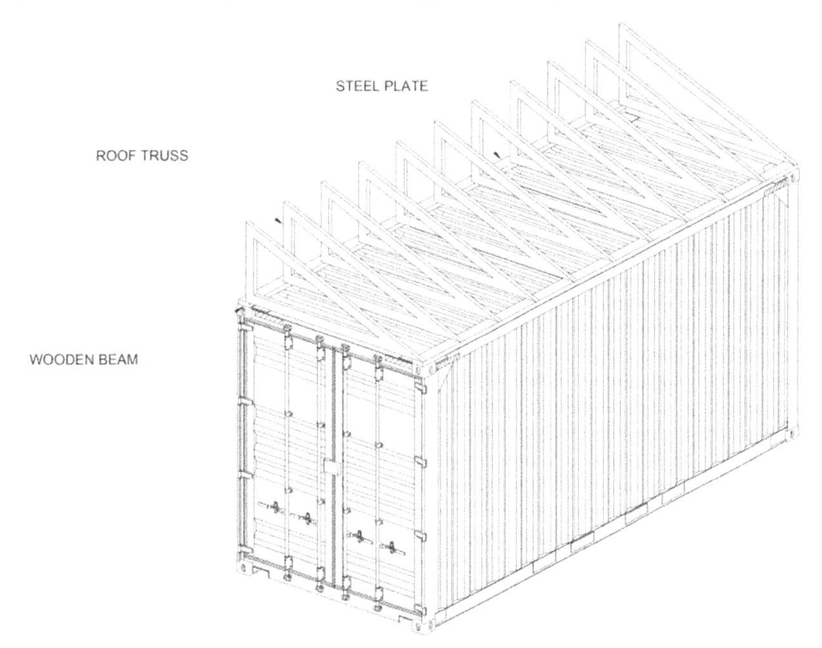

Covering your shed-style roof is the last stage in its construction. This conversion, moreover, can be achieved in several ways. Roofing shingles, coated steel sheets, and galvanized steel sheets are all possibilities. Shingles are the least expensive choice, but they are also the least lasting.

Metal and glass sheets are more robust and less difficult to install.

Coated steel is the most durable choice, but it is also the costliest and requires more equipment and know-how. That' s the option you should go for if you want your structure to last as long as possible, regardless of expense. Examine your choices in terms of money, talents, budget, and timeliness, and you'll be able to choose which roof covering is ideal for you.

The last stage in the shed roof building is to make sure it has enough ventilation. To do so successfully, make sure the trusses overhang the

roof by 1 foot on all sides. Install a fascia board on both lengths of the roof, then a soffit board with a 1-inch gap. For ventilation, to enable airflow while keeping pests out, the wire mesh should be placed over the ventilation gap.

The roof's ventilation system will enable air to circulate freely throughout the whole building. This prevents heat-trapping as well as rust-causing humidity.

Tips: Make sure to check your design with a structural engineer.

They will be able to determine the exact load-bearing requirements of your roof, given the natural stresses imposed by wind, rain, and snow in your region. The number of trusses and purlin placement has been offered as an over-spec recommendation, fitting for most circumstances.

The scheme shown below illustrates the construction of the fascia and soffit board:

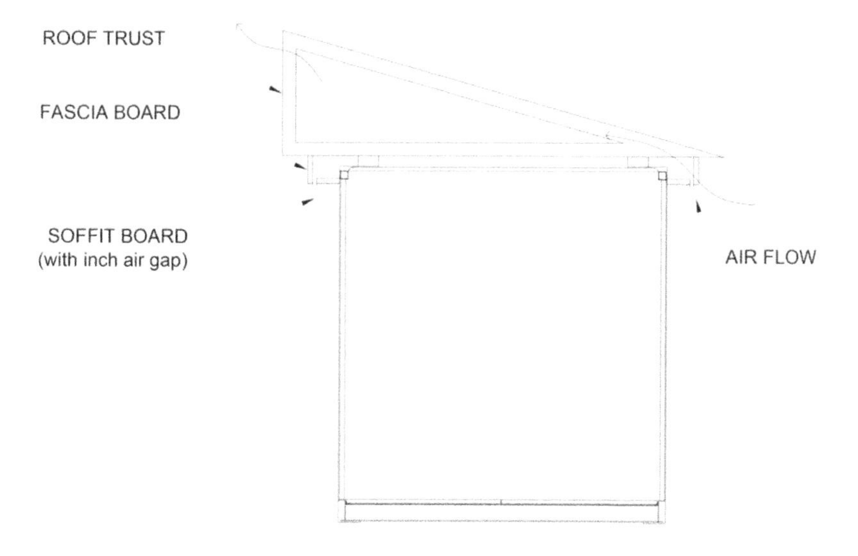

Gable Roof

The gable roof is the next roofing type to consider.

Gable roofs have a peak in the center and slope down to either edge of the building's length. This is a more conventional roof that gives

the house a more attractive appearance and resembles the roof of a classic home.

It has a triangular roof that is excellent for water drainage, extending the life of both the roof and your home. Another benefit of the gabled roof is that it provides much more ceiling area than other roof types. This will not be a problem in most shipping container houses, but it does provide a chance to add additional insulation to your roof.

The diagram below shows the general design of the gable roof:

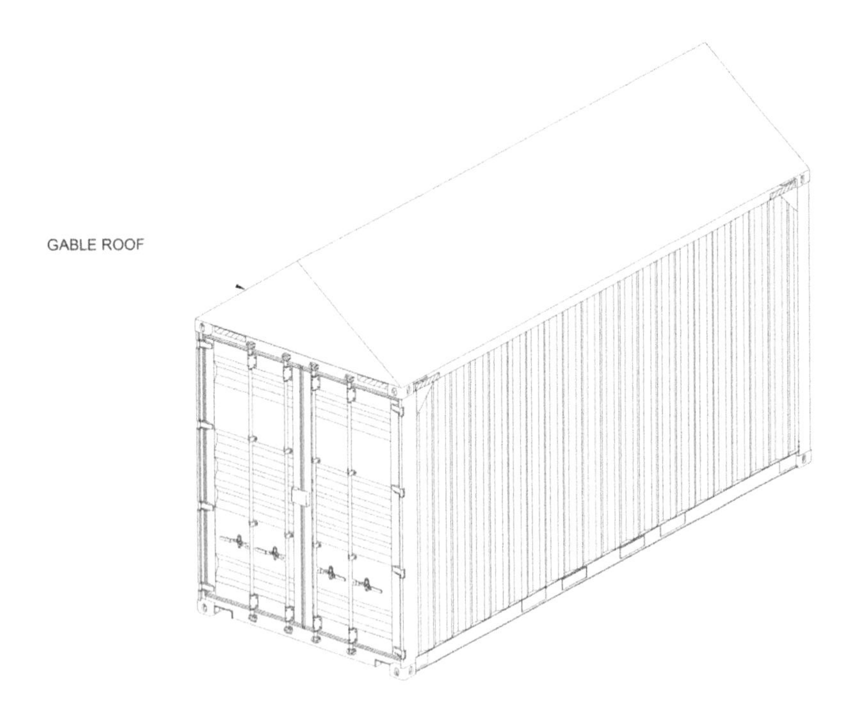

Installation

The installation of the gable roof is similar to that of the shed roof installation. The first step, just as in that of the shed-style roof installation, is to weld a perfect-angled steel play across both lengths of the container.

Once again, the upper flange of the right-angled plate is then used as a base to affix wooden 2x6 beams. Screw or nail the trusses into place using a skew pattern, and place the trusses about 18 in. apart. Affix the purlins with nails or screws, placing them approximately 1 ft. apart. Shingles, galvanized steel plates, or coated sheets of steel can be used to cover the purlins.

Once again, in providing sufficient ventilation, ensure that the trusses overhang the width of the roof by 1 ft. on each side. Install

soffit and fascia boards, providing a 1-inch empty space in the center

of the soffit boards to allow for airflow, and cover these gaps with a mesh of wire. The diagrams below show the construction cross-section of the gable roof and the details which show how to arrange appropriate ventilation:

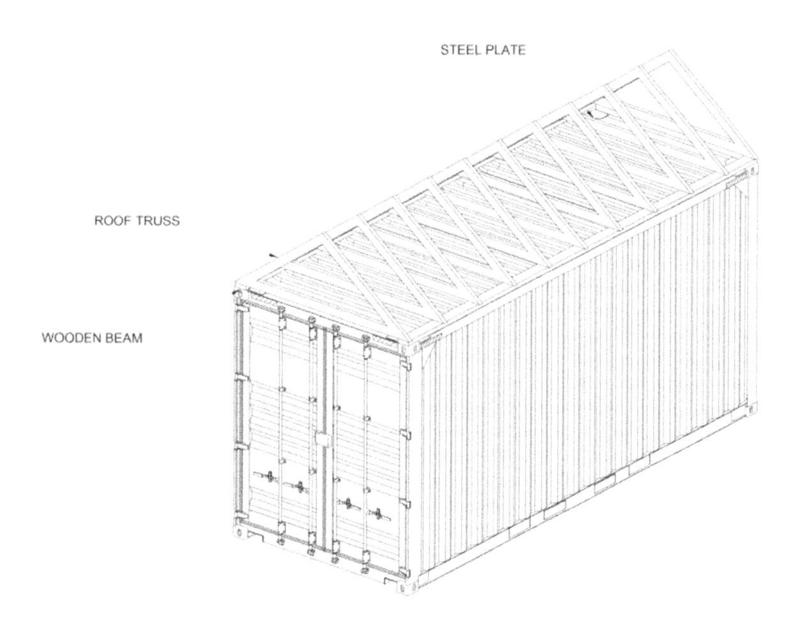

How to arrange appropriate ventilation:

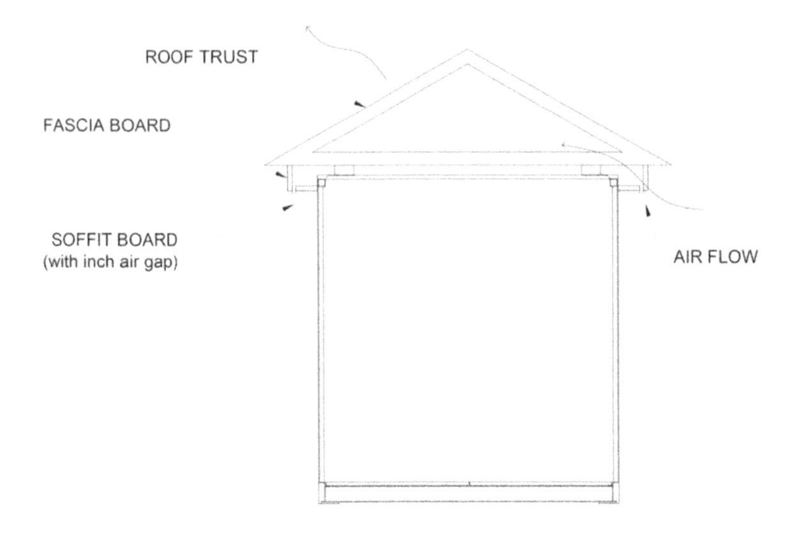

Roofing Checklist

- Consult with a structural engineer about the roofing and load-bearing needs of your home. Take the load-taking capacity of your roof into consideration for your area and the typical weather patterns.
- Decide upon the roofing style for your home.
- Construct your roof.

4.11 Water, electricity, sewage and phone line services

No home is complete without basic services. First fix services involve running the lines for electricity, telephone, sewage, and water into your container. For water, this essentially involves running the main, while sewage involves attaching the drain point(s) and running the line to the sewer or septic tank. With telephone and electricity, the lines are run to the outside of the container and led through the service box into the interior.

Once the first fix services have been established, it will be necessary to take care of flooring, framing the ceiling and interior walls, and placing the insulation.

The second fix services can be placed to ensure that the service lines are run to their desired location in the completed home. This involves light fixtures, light switches, interior electric boxes, faucets, and any other services which must be run through the interior of the home.

Choices about services should be made with consideration of the chosen foundation type. It's important to remember that if you choose a raft or trench foundation, you will need to lay out the lines for water, electricity, sewage, and phone before you lay the foundation. You have a bit more margin if you choose a pier or pile foundation, as you can run the lines for services after placing the container.

To have access to the underground lines for sewage and water, you will need to remove a portion of the flooring. This will not be necessary for electricity and telephone lines, as they can be led into the interior through the wall of the container in the area of your service box.

The diagram for the placement of services should be a part of your initial plan.

You will want to know where your electric service box will go, arrange the bathroom and kitchen so that they are both near the water and sewage line, and generally have an idea of how you will run the electrics so that all rooms have the necessary power and phone access. When designing your home, clearly mark the services plan over the diagram of your home so that you can build accordingly.

Installing Your Services

Remember that all of the services should be clearly marked on your initial design plan. If you have factored them in from the beginning, the installation should be straightforward, and you will save yourself from costly mistakes later in the process. Here are a few details that will help you to think through the process of services installation.

Electric Services

The first question when arranging electric services is where you plan to install your service panel. The electrics can either be run underground to attach to the service box or run along the roof of the containers. If you choose to weld the containers together, then you will be unable to run the electric line down between the containers, so running it underground will be the only option.

In most areas, building regulations require electrics to be run by a certified electrician. First, find out the building regulations for your area. Electricity can be tricky to play with, so unless you are certain that you have the necessary technical know-how, reach out to a local electrician to make sure the cables are run safely. Also remember that shipping containers are metal boxes and that metal conducts electricity very well. Because of this, you will want to ground the line, earthing the whole structure with a grounding rod.

Drill through the structure to attach the service securely, and then run the electric line along the centerline of the home. For first fix services, all that is necessary is to run the electric line to the service

box and then through the wall of the container into the interior.

Second fix services will then involve installing an interior electric box and running power to all desired locations in the house.

For second fix services, you will want to run lines to every planned light fixture and power outlet, ensuring that all rooms have the desired access to electricity.

Run the cables in the areas between the internal studs so that they will be concealed with the interior walls.

The route for your power cable should be clearly marked in the design phase, and the actual installation should be left to a certified electrician.

The diagrams below demonstrate one simple plan for running the electricity to a small dwelling and indicate the method of placing the cable in the space between interior studs. This will be covered more fully in upcoming chapters, which deal with second-fix services.

Sewage Installation

The biggest thing that you need to remember about installing your sewage is that it runs on the force of gravity. This means that you need to allow for a drop between the drains and the run of the pipe away from home. You will have to drill through the bottom of the container to allow space for the pipe to pass through. Run a vertical length of pipe through the drilled hole, and then connect an elbow to direct the flow of sewage toward the outlet. The other end of the line will be run to the sewage outlet. In remote or rural areas, the sewage outlet will be a septic tank, while in urban areas, you will be running your sewage pipes to the main sewer.

Since gravity is the force that drives your sewage, the farther the source of the outlet, the deeper the sewage line will need to be. Also, you will need to ensure that your sewage line is placed below the freeze depth of your area. These are, therefore, the two requirements to be considered when planning the depth of your sewage line.

The general rule is to ensure that the pipe drops ¼ in. per foot of travel. This means that you will need a 1-ft. drop for 48 ft. of travel. The bare minimum of the drop is 1/8 in. per foot, though you will have far fewer problems with the previous recommendation. Additionally, this means that a 2-ft. drop from the drain will reach

96 ft., theoretically. However, due to the resistance caused by horizontal travel, you will probably want to expect it to travel only 75 ft.

Another consideration is based completely upon efficiency. To avoid running two sewage lines distant from one another, you will want to try to arrange your plan so that all drains can empty into the same line.

This means that you will want to make the kitchen and bathroom close to one another in your plan. This is not always possible, especially with more complicated builds. However, it should be considered a central goal in simpler builds.

Water Line Installation

The first step in supplying your house with a water line is to dig a trench to house the pipes. The water pipe should be no less than 14 in. (350 mm) from electricity and other services.

Furthermore, you will want to dig the trench at least 3.5 ft. (750 mm) down. If the frost depth for your area is lower than this, then make sure that the run of your pipe is placed beneath frost depth. Your local planning authority should have the ability to provide you with specifics on the frost depth in your area. Make sure the trench width is no less than 1 ft. (300 mm), providing plenty of space to lay all necessary pipes.

A few other considerations when running your water pipes: first, they should be filled with sand rather than gravel or rubble. The inlet of your water pipe will need to be run to a water main in urban environments and to a well with a pump in more remote settings. You can use the same trench for the water and sewage pipes, and this will save a bit of digging. However, it is unnecessary to ensure that the pipe has a specific fall per foot, as water pressure provides the force which pushes the water through the line.

Telephone Line Services

Just as the sewage and water lines can be run alongside one another, the phone line and electric line can be wired together. Just as with the electric line, the telephone line can be run either through the roof or the bottom of the container. A third option is to drill directly through the container at the location of the service box and lead both the electric and phone lines through at this entrance point.

You will want to seal the entry point well, if you choose this approach. For raft foundations, you will need to install the phone line through the space of the foundation before laying the concrete on the foundation. Regardless of your foundation, it is visually more appealing to run the line beneath the container.

When burying the phone line, remember to keep the trench at least 14 in. (350 mm) away from the waterline. The phone line can be run inside a PVC tube with an inner diameter of 0.8 in. (22 mm). Run the phone line up through the base of the container and then use mastic to seal the holes.

Services Installation Checklist

- Make sure to plan out the services when arranging the initial design.
- Place the service box in the most convenient location for access both inside the container and to the desired areas within the container.
- If possible, plan the drains for the kitchen and bathroom so that they can be close to one another and use a single outlet.
- Arrange the phone line so that it can be laid alongside the electric line.
- Arrange the sewage line so that it can be laid alongside the waterline.
- Ensure that the water line is at least 350 mm (14 in.) from the electric line.
- Place the horizontal runs of pipe below the frost line.
- When laying the sewage, make sure that you have ¼ in. of drop for each foot of travel.

4.12 Flooring

Once you've finished installing your flooring, you're just a few steps away from having a completely functioning house that you can move into and start enjoying as a living place. Dealing with the old flooring and laying the completed flooring are the two main stages in this procedure.

Container flooring basics

Marine plywood is used in most containers. It's tempting to just utilize this as your home's flooring, and in certain instances, this may be feasible. Pesticides and other dangerous chemicals will, however, be used to treat the floors in most containers. As a result, they are unsuited for use as flooring.

If you're purchasing new containers, one option is to talk to the manufacturer about leaving the flooring untreated. You'll need to either remove or cover the flooring with used and one-time-use containers. Pesticides and other chemicals will not harm you or your family if you use either technique. A subfloor or a non-breathable underlay may be used to cover the flooring. Finally, the original flooring may be poured with concrete. We now have four flooring choices to choose from.

Removing Hazardous Flooring

The simplest solution is to remove the containers' current flooring and replace it with new plywood. This is a straightforward procedure, but it may take some time, particularly if you're dealing with many containers. The extra plywood expenses will have to be included in the original budget as well.

If the plywood has holes or other damage, the only solution may be to remove and replace the floor. If you want to skip this procedure, inspecting the flooring of the containers before purchasing them would be beneficial.

It's important to note that this phase must be completed before any inside container work, such as erecting stud walls and framing the interior.

Installing a Subfloor

You may install a subfloor instead of removing the existing flooring if you don't want to remove it. To prevent toxins from seeping through the flooring in vapor form, the first stage in this procedure is to build a barrier over the current flooring.

Cleaning the current flooring with isopropyl alcohol is the first step. After that, apply a low-v epoxy to the floor. In wet or high-moisture environments, low viscosity epoxy performs effectively. It comes in 1.5-gallon packages that cover 150-175 square feet. The floor will be properly sealed after one to two applications. This produces a vapor-tight barrier that successfully keeps dangerous substances contained.

The epoxy coating may then be covered with 34-inch marine plywood. This is when tongue and groove plywood sheets come in handy. 2-in. coated deck screws may be pushed straight through the top layer and into the old flooring to secure the new flooring.

Before installing the new plywood, a 1/2-inch layer of foam may be applied over the epoxy barrier. Additional insulation will be provided as a result of this. It is important to note, however, that installing a subfloor costs one inch of height. This alternative is equally as expensive as ripping out the old flooring and installing new.

Non-Breathable Flooring Underlay

The last option for dealing with the flooring is to use an underlayment. This absolutely is the most affordable choice. This may also be done after constructing the inside and before laying the final flooring. It's also easy to lay, taking the shortest amount of time of any technique.

The first step in putting down an underlay is the same as putting down a subfloor. The old flooring should be cleaned before applying a low-v epoxy coating. Cut the underlayment to size and form after that. Place over the existing flooring and secure with nails through the underlayment.

Concrete Flooring

There are several advantages in having a concrete floor, but it also has some drawbacks. The original maritime plywood may be immediately poured with concrete. It may be used as a completed flooring after it has been installed and finished. It's long-lasting and simple to clean, and it may be colored, polished, or adorned with a pattern for added appeal.

In terms of disadvantages, concrete has a tendency to accumulate cold. Thus, it may not be suitable in colder regions. It will make

keeping the house warm more difficult, and it may be unpleasant to walk on. Additionally, 2 mm thick steel bars will need to be welded across the length and breadth of the chamber before pouring the concrete. The bars should be welded one inch above the ground level and spaced one foot apart.

The last stage is to pour and finish the concrete once the steel bars have been welded in place. The last disadvantage is that you must wait for the concrete to dry before proceeding with the inside work.

4.13 Finishing the Flooring

The new floor may be customized in a variety of ways. Concrete, tile, laminate, and carpet are all options. If you choose concrete, both the subflooring and the flooring are done at the same time. In hotter regions, concrete, tile, and laminate are excellent since they assist in keeping the home cool. Carpet will be more beneficial in cooler temperatures. The location of carpet, tile, and laminate will be discussed in the sections below.

The first step in installing any kind of flooring is to measure the area to be covered. To determine how much carpet, how many tiles, or how many pieces of the laminate you'll need, you'll need the entire square footage of the floor area. You'll also have to know the measurements of each room so that the carpet can be trimmed to fit and the tiles or laminate can be split appropriately.

Laying Carpet

Carpet is more difficult to maintain than tile, concrete, or laminate, but it is softer on the feet and helps to keep the house warm. It's also a little simpler to set up.

The first stage in carpet installation is to use a carpet gripper to line the space's walls. Carpet grippers are just thin strips of wood with sharp pins projecting from one end. The carpet will be held in place with these pegs. A carpet gripper should be used to line all inside walls of the house where the carpet will be installed.

It's critical to allow a 10 mm space between the wall and the carpet gripper's wall edge. To cut the carpet gripper to size, use tinsnips. The carpet may then be hammered down or adhered to the floor using carpet gripper adhesive.

After that, you'll need to put down your carpet underlay. This is a rubber-and-foam layer underneath the carpet that offers comfort. It must be installed inside the carpet grippers. Fit one edge of the underlay to the carpet gripper against one wall, then roll out until you reach the other wall, with the rubber side down. Cut the underlay snugly against the carpet gripper of this wall using a utility knife. Rep to this procedure until you've covered the whole area with underlay and sealed the seams with carpet tape.

The last step is to install the carpet. To begin, cut the carpet to the room's size. Then, loosely spread it down in the room, making sure one corner is in place. Make your way to the opposite corner, aligning each one precisely. Because the carpet will stretch somewhat when fitted on the grippers, leave an additional 50 mm at each edge.

It's crucial to start on the wall opposite the entryway when installing your carpet. Place the carpet on the grippers and make sure it's flat. Cut away any extra material with a utility knife as you work rearward towards the entrance.

Laying Floor Tiles

The tile is simple to maintain and may be very attractive. It's perfect for hotter areas since it helps to keep the home cool. Because the areas for most basic designs will be rectangular, laying tile in a shipping container house is very easy. If you choose to frame the exterior facing walls before installing tile, you have greatly simplified the tile installation procedure. If not, you'll have to be able to accurately cut the tiles to fill the area for the corrugated walls.

Depending on the geometry of the space and the tile design, you may lay tile in a variety of ways. One of the easiest is to use chalk lines to mark the center of the room and move outward from there. This will give the center a beautiful appearance, but it will need cutting the tiles that run up to the walls.

Another alternative is to start with one wall and work your way to the other wall, one row at a time. If you're going to put color patterns in your tile, you may want to start in the center. You should experiment with a few different dry layouts to see which one works best in the area you're tiling.

Spread thin-set mortar or floor tile adhesive over your chosen starting point, keying it in with the flat side of a notched trowel and then lining it into grooves with the notched side. Because thinnest and glue dry fast, cover just a small area before installing tile.

Place the first tile and firmly push it into place, then add tile spacers to the corners. Continue placing tiles, each one fitting into the spaces before it.

Use a spirit level to check if the tiles are level with one another from time to time. Working your way up to the room's boundaries, save the odd spots near the wall for last. You'll be able to measure and cut all of the incomplete tiles in one go. You'll want to back butter the partial tiles and place them in the remaining places.

Allow for a 24-hour cure time if using a thin-set. Wait until the thin-set has cured before putting any weight on the freshly placed tiles. Ceramic tile adhesive has a much shorter cure time, which will be specified by the manufacturer. Remove the spacers, then fill the gaps with grout once the thin-set or glue has dried. Cover tiny areas of the tile with grout at a time, then rinse the tile clean. Grout sealant should be applied to the grooves.

Tips for professional-looking tile: It is not recommended to tile directly onto plywood. While it is possible, it may result in uneven tiles, and the adhesive or thin-set may not adhere well. Instead, you can place a layer of the concrete board over the plywood. The concrete board will provide a smooth surface to keep the tiles even.

Lay the concrete board down so that the joints between the boards alternate. Screw the concrete board into the plywood flooring, countersinking the screw heads flush with the surface of the concrete board. Tape and mud the joints between concrete boards. This can then be used as a surface to lay tile.

Another key consideration is whether to use thin-set mortar or ceramic tile adhesive. Tile adhesive is easier to work with; however, there are a few drawbacks.

First, it is only slightly water-resistant. In the event of high-water conditions, the adhesive will begin to mold and lose adhesive properties. The adhesive is also not recommended for high-traffic conditions.

Thinnest mortar is preferable for floors, as you will be able to fill voids and ensure that the tiles are level. It is also more water-resistant and will result in a more durable tile floor. Tile cement is preferable for vinyl and linoleum tiles, while the thin-set mortar is best for ceramic and porcelain tile.

If using an alternating color pattern, arrange the boxes beforehand so that you know which to pull from when laying.

This is especially important if you would like to arrange the tiles in a pattern. This can be tricky, so if you are laying tile for the first time, it may be best to use a simple layout.

Lay down only as much mortar or adhesive as you can work within ten minutes, and then lay down more once you have covered this and added spacers.

Laying Laminate Flooring

Laminate flooring may be installed directly over the original plywood or over a non-breathable underlay. If you want to put the flooring first before constructing the container, start at the left-hand corner of each container. If you've already framed the container, you may start in the left-hand corner of each room, opposite the entrance.

Place the next board end-on to the preceding after the first has been placed. Slide the board down at a 30-degree angle, then drop the other end into position, squeezing the ends together as you bring it flat and secure it. Continue to place boards until the first row is complete, trimming the last piece to length if required. Laying the last piece over the preceding and marking the required length is a simple way to do this. After cutting following the markings, place the last board in the empty area.

One of the most important aspects in installing a a long-lasting laminate floor is to stage the seams. To start the next row of laminate, you'll need to cut a fresh board in half. Slide the sliced edge against the wall and into the preceding row. It's possible that the last row of planks may need to be trimmed down to size. By placing the piece length-wise over the preceding row and noting the width that remains, the length may be measured in the same way as the end-board.

If you frame the container before you lay the laminate, it will be much simpler to do so. Otherwise, you'll have to cut the laminate boards surrounding the container's corrugated walls. This is a time-consuming and delicate process, with missed cuts potentially resulting in material waste.

To show how laminate boards lock together, look at the picture below:

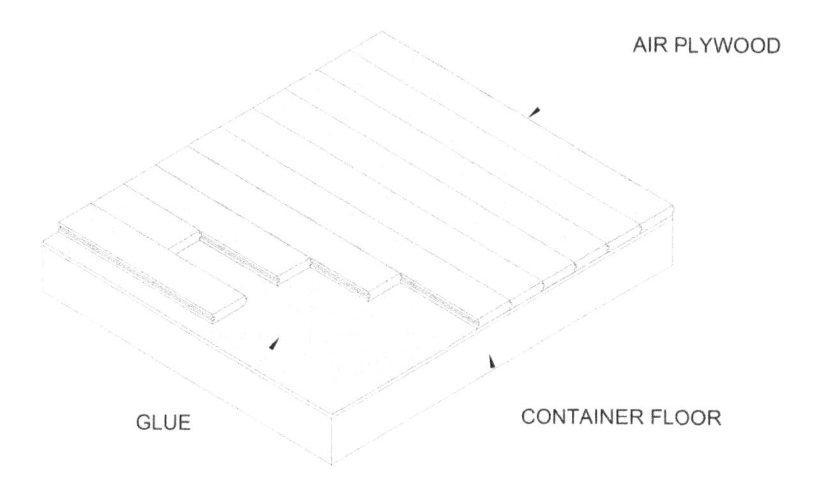

Flooring – Checklist

- If you are ordering a new container, request that it be constructed with the floors untreated with chemicals.
- Either remove the original flooring or fix any damaged areas.
- Decide on your subflooring. Either remove old plywood and replace new, cover the existing plywood with a non-breathable underlay, use a non-breathable underlay and add a subfloor or lay concrete flooring.
- Decide on the finished flooring. Options include tile, laminate, carpet, or concrete. Keep the climate in mind. Carpet is better for colder climates, while tile, laminate, and concrete are better in warmer climates.

Remember that a concrete board subfloor is recommended if laying tile.

4.14 Finishing interior walls

The the floor, the walls and the ceiling are all made of the same material. This is the house's shell, the components that give your new home its overall vibe. You do, however, have certain choices, just as you have with any other element of house building. The most conventional method is to hang drywall and then paint it. If you want to install a veneer plaster wall, you may dress up the drywall with plaster. A thin wood veneer may also be applied to the drywall. Textured wall panels are another option.

If you don't want to use drywall, you may use genuine wood paneling or even plywood instead. Wahoo walls or basement wall finishing systems are two examples of pre-made wall panels that may be utilized. Another alternative is to utilize a plaster and lath method, which takes longer but is more durable and visually appealing. Hundreds of horizontal wood slats are placed and plastered over in this process.

Only two of these techniques will be discussed in this section: real wood walls and painted drywall. However, once you grasp the concepts underlying these two, the rest of the methods will be self-explanatory.

Painted Drywall

Drywall is one of the more efficient materials for creating a support surface for stud walls. It is inexpensive and may be embellished in a variety of ways. The drywall is basically measured, cut, and fitted against the stud walls before being painted over.

Preparation

Cleaning the space and covering the freshly installed flooring should be the first steps. Make sure there are no obstacles in the way of reaching the floor or ceiling. Drop cloths should be used to avoid spills and drips. Place painter's tape around electrical switches or outlets, door frames, windows, or any other places you don't want to get paint on. You may also designate a space for paint mixing and gear storage.

The the shop assistant will be able to assist you with your paint purchase. They'll be able to recommend the right brush or roller for the task, as well as the many finishes available. The roller's substance will also be determined by the paint's composition. Synthetic brushes are required for water-based and latex paints, whereas natural brushes are required for alkyd and oil-based paints.

Before applying the paint, give it a good shake and mix it with a piece of wood. If you're using multiple paint cans, combine them in a tub before painting to ensure that the color is consistent.

Before painting, clean the drywall of any dust or debris. Close all doors and windows and use a dehumidifier if you're working in a wet environment.

Proceed from the top to the bottom. If you're starting with the ceiling, work your way up to the tops of the walls before lowering the roller to the floor. If you won't paint the ceiling, start at the tops of the walls and work your way down to the floor. Remember to use painter's tape to seal the joint between the walls and the ceiling.

When using a roller to paint, make long strokes that go from top to bottom. At the halfway point of the preceding roller stripe, place the next one. The thickness and hue will be constant as a result of this. In addition, rather than trying a few heavy coats, you should apply many light layers of paint. This will result in a more uniform and pleasing appearance.

Once the paint has dry, remove the painter's tape. Before removing the tape, use a hair drier to weaken the adhesive. Trim the remaining area with tiny brushes after the tape has been removed, being careful not to paint beyond the intended boundary.

Real Wood Walls

The use of real wood as an alternative to drywall is a viable option. If you wish to use genuine wood to cover your stud walls, you need first use Visqueen to cover the insulation-filled stud walls. Stretch

the Visqueen over the wall and secure it with nails to the studs. After you've installed the plastic sheet, you can start applying your real-wood finish to the stud walls.

There are several choices for genuine wood walls, but tongue-and-groove pine slats are one that will illustrate the concept. Working from the floor to the ceiling, start slapping the slats against the studs. Fix the slats to the studs and stagger the joints. This is, in essence, a straightforward application. You'll need to trim each board to length after measuring the extra length. In the same way, the last row will need to be trimmed to width.

This will provide a lovely wall finish with a log cabin vibe. It's one of the most basic and yet visually appealing finishes you can give your house, and it's very straightforward to do, even with limited equipment and abilities.

Finishing Interior Walls – Checklist

- Choose the finish for your interior walls. You may opt for painted drywall, paneling, drywall veneer, real wood, or the other options mentioned above. If choosing to use painted drywall, prepare the drywall to receive paint and prepare the area to protect it from spillage or excess paint by using drop cloths and painters' tape. After the paint has dried, trim the edges of walls and around light switches and power outlets.
- If choosing to panel the walls with real wood, stagger the joints and line the edges up with the battens. Remember that drywall is unnecessary for this design option.

Chapter 5

How to make containers self-sufficient

A self-sufficient house may seem like a wonderful concept, but are you uncertain what it entails or what it looks like in reality?

It's straightforward. There are a few requirements that self-sustained households must fulfill to be called self-sustained. Here's a list of them:

Must produce energy

A self-contained dwelling should be able to generate its own energy. This may be accomplished via solar electricity, wind power, or a combination of the two.

Recognize that this will be a long-term commitment and solar and wind energy systems are not cheap.

Current solar systems include a battery that is connected to your home. Solar panels harness the sun's energy to generate electricity. The battery gets charged to the point that it can power your house for the whole day.

Excess energy is sold to your electric provider in exchange for a bill credit. You may take electricity from your electric provider if you don't generate enough energy for the day due to the weather.

Water must come from the property

A self-contained house should have access to its own water supply. You may either have a well on your property or collect rainwater.

Having a well is probably the easiest solution, but it is not always possible. Rainwater may, however, be collected and a rainwater collecting system installed. These systems are made up of rain collection and storage devices.

Gutters may be attached to the side of your house and used to feed big barrels. The water should then be pushed through the system to maintain adequate water pressure.

To make the water safe to drink, you'll need a filtering system. You may also utilize a solar-heated hot water tank to heat the water for showers and laundry.

Keep in mind that greywater is present in every household. Because it includes food particles, soap particles, and hair that falls down the drain when bathing, most houses have a method for this water to be pumped out of the house and securely drained away from the property.

However, you may use a rainwater collecting system to recycle greywater as well. It may be used to irrigate your plants and then filtered a third time before being flushed in your home's toilets.

To minimize the quantity of trash produced by the house, a self-sufficient household will find out how to reuse what it generates many times.

Manage waste

It is mentioned above about greywater, which brings us to the subject of waste. If you wish to live in a self-sufficient house, you'll need to figure out how to dispose of your trash.

Toilets may be connected to a septic system, and the water used to flush the toilets could be filtered greywater.

You might, however, try utilizing a composting toilet. This is a toilet that is not connected to the sewage system. You use the restroom, and the trash is sorted and composted.

Must have a way to provide heat

A self-sufficient house must be able to generate its own heat. Traditional heating and air systems may be fueled by solar or wind energy.

However, there are also other heat sources that can be considered. For example, by utilizing a wood-burning stove or putting a water stove in your house, you may have your own alternative heat source.

The water stove heats and heats water in your house by burning tiny quantities of wood.

A wood stove is a fantastic source of heat and a backup cooking stove in the event that your alternate power source fails.

You may also construct a barrel woodstove for a low cost as a backup or for additional warmth during the winter months.

Must be built from recycled products

If you're thinking of constructing a self-contained home, keep in mind that it should be constructed entirely of recycled materials. This may imply that the house was constructed using renewable materials, locally obtained materials, or by upcycling other people's garbage.

Cob dwellings or a green roof for your self-sustaining home, should also be considered. These are both ecological alternatives that put nature to work rather than contributing to landfills.

Consider going a step farther and utilizing recycled materials as insulation. Many people are replacing conventional insulation with straw bales in their walls. They are a natural substance that does an excellent job of preserving heat and cold.

There are many options for building a more environmentally friendly and efficient house. It will require some investigation into what goods are accessible in your region.

However, once you've found them, your dream house might be only a few ideas away from being a reality.

Pros and cons of self-sustained house

Building a self-sufficient house, like everything else, has advantages and disadvantages. The following are some of the benefits:

You may live a self-sustaining lifestyle and be prepared in the event of a catastrophe that disrupts your present way of life, even if just for a short time. (For example, natural catastrophes.)

You should be able to enjoy a bill-free existence after your systems are in place and paid for. This gives you and your family financial independence.

Living in a self-sufficient house has just one major disadvantage. Many people's finances are unable to manage the initial expenses. It may take some time to save and construct a home in this design.

However, once you've mastered the capacity to construct, you'll be well on your way to being debt-free and self-sufficient.

5.1 How to transform your current home

Many people may read this and think to themselves, "This sounds great, but I don't have the money, I'm not willing to relocate out of my present location, and I suppose these rules me out of having a self-sufficient house".

"Don't give up!" I tell you. This already happened to someone else, and now I'm going to show you some low-cost steps by which you'll be able to reach your goals, whatever your starting condition is.

So, if you have to remain in your present house for whatever reason, consider adding the following things to your current living situation:

- A vegetable garden to feed your family
- In your present position, try to utilize less energy.
- Start looking at alternative energy options for your house.
- Improve your existing living condition by adding wood heat.
- To grow food, add a tiny greenhouse.
- Invest in a flock of chickens for meat and eggs.
- Collect rainwater on your property to use for watering plants, animals, or cleaning.

There are many options for living a self-sufficient existence exactly where you are. You may have to think outside the box, and you may have to save for bigger, self-sustaining items for a time, but it will be worth it in the end.

Not only are you becoming more self-sufficient, but it may also add value to your house in many instances.

You may discover even more methods to make your present or future house self-sufficient. Hopefully, this will serve as a starting point for you since although living a self-sufficient lifestyle requires more effort, it is also very gratifying.

Chapter 6

Design ideas and creative ways to save space

Saving and gaining space

Working with one container as your home is going to prove challenging. You will have to change the way you look at a home and envision how everything will fit without your home ending up feeling cramped.

Here are some things you should consider:

1. The living area – do you really need this inside your house?
2. Bedroom – Think about how much time you spend in your bedroom every day.
3. Kitchen – How big of a kitchen do you need?
4. Dining area – If you live alone, do you really need a place dedicated to dining only?
5. Toilet and bath – How much space do you need to take care of your basic hygiene?

For the living area:

A solution to widening your space is to install a patio and large doors that open up to them. This, in effect, opens up your whole house, making it feel less cramped. This can become your living room where you can entertain guests. The added cost to create a deck should be minimal as you will only need to install a metal stage for wooden planks to rest on, and you will now have that magnificent deck that your guests can admire and enjoy.

For the bedroom:

Many container homes use loft-type bedrooms to answer their space-saving issues.

Another solution to this is to use dual-purpose furniture. For example, there are companies that specialized in creating furniture that tucks away when not needed. A bed, when not used, is just taking up space. So why not transform that space into a usable one during your waking hours. A wall bed or a Murphy bed is an excellent solution to space issues inside a 20-foot container home.

For the kitchen and dining area:

You can have your kitchen and dining area share the same space. Not only is this an efficient way to save space, but you'll most likely be eating food you prepared instantly near or in your kitchen anyway. So, what you will mainly need is a sink and a work area to prepare your food.

You can also use tables that can be stowed away when not in use.

Another thing that you will have to put into consideration with regards to your kitchen is the size of your appliances. Not only that, you'll have to make a crucial decision as to what appliances you'll really need. So, we need a refrigerator to store food in and an electric stove to cook food in. Other than that, you won't need much more.

For the toilet and bath:

Ample space should be provided to allow you to move freely inside your toilet and bath so you'll be able to clean yourself thoroughly. There is no point in making a toilet and bath which is too small to use, so think of how much space you'd want it to take up in your container home. For most container homes, this is the only room that is particularly sealed off from the rest of the place. As a basic standard, a toilet and bath which is 4 feet wide and 4 feet deep should be enough to make your bathroom nice to use. In fact, others have even gone smaller than that, but you'll have to take into consideration of your height and body size as well. In the future, you can get that extra 10-footer container van and just dedicate it to becoming a bathroom if you choose to do so.

Design ideas

Walls

You can use plywood for your interior walls to hide the metal from sight and make it feel cozier. Use marine-grade plywood, which is at least half an inch thick for your walls.

That way, you won't punch holes through them accidentally.

Afterward, you can paint it in whatever color you choose.

Floors

If you've ever run through or walked over metal, then you're already familiar with that clunking sound. Over time this can be annoying, and to avoid this in your own home, install some floors.

By using standard 2 x 2 long pieces of wood, you'll be able to create a raised space inside your home. This is also an excellent place to hide unsightly wires. The next step is to top off the basic framework of your floors with high-quality planks, which you can purchase off a mall.

Windows

The bigger your windows are, the more light will flow into your home. So this should be high up on your list to install in your home. Some container homes even feature slit-type windows near the top to ensure light coming in while minimizing the breach of privacy. A good idea for your container home is to dedicate a place for floor-to-ceiling windows that are narrow enough to provide privacy and yet large enough to allow natural light to enter.

Installing normal windows that you can swing out for air to come into your home is something you should also consider.

Doors

As seen in previous chapters, container homes often feature narrow hallways. In this case, you'll need to ensure that your doors won't get in the way of your movements inside. A good suggestion is to use sliding doors. Instead of swinging in or out, the doors will just slide to allow ingress and egress easily.

Another good option is to use accordion doors which most RVs and mobile homes use.

Plastic or faux wood

In the interest of saving money and extending the life of your interior, you can substitute wood with plastic planks. These are commercially available.

Another plus factor for this is that they're quite varied in their appearance

They're also very easy to clean, so that should be something worth considering.

Tip: It'll be a good idea to look at what industry leaders have done to mobile homes and RVs to give you an idea of how to save space further in regards to your interior. Use their knowledge to your advantage in creating the perfect interior for your container home.

Chapter 7
Exterior finishes

The outside of your container may be finished in a variety of ways, just like the rest of the procedure. Whether or not you have insulated the outside of your container is one of the most important factors in this procedure. Even if you have put foam insulation on the outside of the container, you will be able to complete the exterior with cladding, but it will be much more difficult and will damage your insulation. As a result, depending on the insulation of the outside, below are some suggested techniques for completing the exterior of your house.

Finishing an Exterior with External Insulation

If you've installed spray foam insulation on the outside of your house, you just have a few choices. The first step is to paint, and the second is to stucco the insulation. You'll want to make sure your insulation is covered and sealed in either case. When sunlight is exposed to closed-cell polyurethane, it starts to deteriorate. Paint or stucco can keep your insulation in good condition and maintain its integrity.

Painting Exterior Insulation

Remember to use latex or water-based acrylic paint when painting over external insulation. Oil-based paints may harm the insulating foam. High-gloss paints should be avoided since they will draw attention to any imperfections in the underlying surface. Paints that are flat or semigloss will assist in concealing the insulation while also providing an attractive appearance.

Before you start painting, take a stroll around the container and look for any rough edges. Suppose any rough edges are visible; smooth them down with sandpaper. To prevent inhaling insulation particles, remember to use a facemask throughout the procedure.

After you've eliminated all of the rough edges, you may paint the outside. Apply three coats at the very least. It's easy to apply using a spray gun, a roller, or a thick brush. Spray guns are the fastest and most consistent way to apply paint. Before starting to apply the paint, be sure to test the flow on scrap cardboard. Rollers will be a little slower, but they will get the job done. Paintbrushes provide the most control, but the results are the slowest.

Tips: You may choose to apply a wax sealant to cover the paint once it has been applied. You will have a better finish if you use several thin coats rather than a single or few thick coats. Before applying a new one, make sure each layer has dried first.

Plastering or Stuccoing the Exterior

If you choose to stucco the exterior of your home, it is best to first ensure that the spray foam insulation has been applied with a rough finish. This will ensure that the surface has more texture for the stucco to grip. Since the render is just for the finish, there's no need to go overboard with it. You can simply purchase just-add-water mixes.

Each 20kg bag will offer 5 mm of cover to a 2.5 m2 (50 ft2) of surface area.

The first step in applying stucco to your home is to fix beading to the corners with adhesive, ensuring that the beading is straight. Cover the ground around the exterior of your home with thick plastic sheets. Mix the stucco powder in a bucket with water, and allow it to stand for five minutes.

While waiting, wet the external insulation down with a hose, providing a damp surface for the stucco to affix to.

Begin applying the stucco from the bottom of the container and work upwards, using a steel trowel. Use long strokes to ensure that it is applied evenly across the surface. Make sure that all stucco is applied within 30 minutes after mixing. As with paint, it is better to place the stucco in multiple thin layers rather than a few thick ones. Try to keep each layer about 5 mm. Rake each layer after application and while still wet. This will offer grip for the next layer. Finish the last layer with a polystyrene float, giving a nice finish to the stucco.

Finishing an Exterior without External Insulation

If you've decided to leave them outside of your container house uninsulated, there are a few options for finishing it. Leaving it naked is one of the simplest, easiest, and cheapest options. This displays the origins of your house and can be both visually appealing and a concrete sign of your accomplishments in the construction of your home.

If, on the other hand, you prefer to enrich it with some finishing touches, you may paint it or cover it with wood. Because leaving the containers unpainted would be meaningless, the next parts will go through the painting and wood cladding processes.

Painting your Container

While keeping your container bare may leave a history about its origins, it also makes it vulnerable to the weather. You can protect your house against rust and extend its life by applying a coat of paint.

The very first step is to have your containers ready. Remove any stickers and wipe the containers' surfaces. If removing the stickers by hand proves impossible, a razor blade may be used. Remove any remaining rust using sandpaper, grinders, or wire brushes if necessary. You should also use thick plastic sheets to cover the ground around your container.

Alkyd enamel paint is the finest exterior paint to use. Brushes, rollers, and spray guns may all be used to apply this to the outside. Spray guns, as previously said, are the quickest choice and offer the most uniform coverage. Rollers are a little slower, but they can still provide a constant level of coverage. Paintbrushes provide the greatest control, but they also need the most expertise to apply consistently. When applying exterior paint, apply three coats at the very least.

Timber Cladding your Exterior

The final option that we will explore is cladding it with timber. This offers an aesthetically pleasing option, giving your home the external appearance of a wood home. It is light and quick to fit, and it can also provide an additional layer of protection to the exterior of your home.

The first step in timber cladding your home is to fit the battens: 2 x 4 in. planks are ideal for this process, and it is best to fit them to the size of the container before framing your container.

Fit the battens 400 mm (16 in.) apart.

Fix them to the container by drilling a hole through the end of each batten 1 ft. from both floor and roof.

Drive a bolt through this hole and tighten a bolt on the inside of the container to hold the batten in place.

After the battens have been affixed at the top and bottom, drill a hole in each foot and repeat the process, tightening a screw on the inside of the container for each one.

The battens will be attached to the container securely.

Once your battens are in place around the perimeter of the container, you will be able to attach cladding to them. Cladding is essentially wooden boards nailed onto the exterior battens. The process is essentially the same as adding real wood to the interior walls. Nail the cladding into the battens using stainless steel nails. Begin at the bottom of the battens and work your way up to the top. Overlap the joints of the cladding as shown in the figure below. Once the cladding has been placed, treat it with a moisture and UV resistant coating.

Finishing Your Exterior – Checklist

- Select your desired exterior, keeping in mind the preferable options for insulated and uninsulated exteriors.
- If you choose to paint an exterior without insulation, make sure to remove all stickers and rust.
- If you choose to paint an insulated exterior, use latex or water-based acrylic paints.
- If you choose to paint an exterior without insulation, use alkyd enamel paints. Use a minimum of three coats. Remember that many thin layers of paint will produce a better finish than a few thick layers.
- For cladding your exterior with timber, begin by lining the exterior with battens.
- Drill holes through the top and bottom of each batten and the container behind it. Drive bolts through the holes and thread a nut on the bolt on the inside of the container.
- Line the battens with wood, going from the bottom up and alternating the edges on different battens.
- Seal the cladding with moisture and UV-resistant sealant.

Thank you for reading Shipping Container Homes!

If you enjoyed this book, I would be grateful if you could take a minute of your time to share it with me by leaving a review.

I think your opinion can help other people find the right solution to their problems, and helps me find new suggestions to offer you content that always fits your needs.

Oliver Tomecek

Scan the QR code to leave a review

Conclusion

The entire process of building a shipping container home can seem very overwhelming. To keep a little peace of mind, remember that once you get the container on your land, you have a semi-complete structure right off the bat. You have four walls and a roof on top of your head, and your belongings will be safe from the weather. Everything else is simply improving your situation. It will be a lot of work, but you can take your time and make your shipping container home perfect for you.

The most important takeaway of this book should be that planning is key. You aren't relying on an architect or engineer to design this house for you. If you aren't utilizing a general contractor to oversee the actual construction of your home, you've chosen to do this yourself, and that means you have to do the thinking and the planning. You may not know how to do everything or even be able to, but you need to know what is supposed to happen. It doesn't matter if you're doing it yourself or hiring someone, you should always know what should happen and verify that what happens in reality always matches your expectations.

If you're feeling a bit overwhelmed, you are not alone. Construction professionals make good money building houses for a reason. The average person either does not know how or is unwilling to undertake such a big project. However, by reading this book, you now know that building a shipping container home is possible. You know that the inside construction of the home is basically the same as a traditional home. You also know you can do much of the work yourself and save money doing so. And when you've finished, you can reflect on the fun parts and the frustrating parts. Future improvements to your property will continue, but that's all they will be: tweaks to be made over time.

Shipping container homes address the problem that affordable housing is becoming increasingly hard to find. By figuring out your minimal living requirements, shipping container homes offer a way to downsize your housing to fit your budget. You can skip the realtors that want to sell you a house that makes you get a second job. You can find a piece of land and a small shipping container and buy all the materials on a minimal budget. You can rest easy in your new shipping container home, knowing that you aren't drowning in debt.

For all the cost savings shipping container homes can provide, they also give a new realm of creativity and unique architecture to those who aren't simply looking to save money. Large homes consisting of multiple containers, sometimes stacked and facing many different directions, can provide their own unique advantages of luxurious living with a tough, weather-resistant shipping container shell. For some, the appeal is being able to take your shipping container home to a new location whenever they want; for others, it's the idea of using old shipping containers and preventing them from going to waste.

Beyond being used for homes, shipping containers have many other uses, like storage buildings. Shipping containers can even be used as small camping cabins, where you simply need a roof over your head.

Shipping container homes are an innovative way for DIY builders to create affordable and unique housing. In this book, we explored the benefits and drawbacks and helped you chart your journey toward building one. Shipping container homes are likely to become more popular, and this book aims to help you join the trend. I hope this guide will help you along the path to your new dream home and that you enjoyed it. Now all that's left is to wish you the best of luck on the rest of your journey for your shipping container home!

Made in the USA
Las Vegas, NV
15 November 2023

80742812R00075